90

*A Conscientious Objector's Journey of Quiet
Resistance*

Bruce Jay Wasser

with Fern Schumer Chapman

GUSSIE ROSE PRESS

Contents

Other books by Fern Schumer Chapman

- *Brothers, Sisters, Strangers: Sibling Estrangement and the Road to Reconciliation*
- *Motherland: A Mother/Daughter Journey to Reclaim the Past*
- *Is it Night or Day?*
- *Middle School Sleuths: How an Eighth-Grade Class Reunited Two Holocaust Refugees*
- *Facing the Past: A Public Memorial Compels a Small German Town to Confront Its History*
- *Three Stars in the Night Sky: A Holocaust Family's Odyssey of Separation and Reunion*
- *Happy Harper Thursdays: A Grandmother's Love for Her Granddaughter during the Coronavirus*
- *The Return of Happy Harper Thursdays: The Guiding Light of a Grandmother's Love*

For more information, please visit: www.fernschumerchapman.com

Cover: IanDagnall Computing/Alamy Photo '69 Draft Lottery

Publisher's Cataloging-in-Publication Data
Names: Wasser, Bruce Jay, author. | Chapman, Fern Schumer, author.
Title: 90 : a conscientious objector's journey of quiet resistance / Bruce Jay Wasser with Fern Schumer Chapman.
Description: Lake Bluff, IL: Gussie Rose Press, 2024.
Identifiers: LCCN: 2024922803 | ISBN: 978-1-962817-11-0 (epub), 978-1-962817-12-7 (paperback)
Subjects: LCSH Wasser, Bruce Jay. | Vietnam War, 1961-1975--Conscientious objectors--United States. |
Vietnam War, 1961-1975--Personal narratives, American. | BISAC BIOGRAPHY & AUTOBIOGRAPHY /
Memoirs | BIOGRAPHY & AUTOBIOGRAPHY / Military | BIOGRAPHY & AUTOBIOGRAPHY / Jewish |
BIOGRAPHY & AUTOBIOGRAPHY / Educators
Classification: LCC DS559.8.C63 W37 2024 | DDC 959.704/3373/092--dc23

For my father, Joe Wasser

"War will exist until that distant day when the conscientious objector enjoys the same reputation and prestige that the warrior does today."

— John F. Kennedy, in a letter he wrote while serving in the Navy in the 1940s.

DECEMBER 1969

"Come on... come on, start! Dammit, *start! Please!*"

I'm begging for cooperation from an industrial dishwasher. Ridiculous, I know — but I'm far past reason in waiting for this monster machine to work. Tonight of all nights, it won't — it *can't* — hold me up.

My evening routine never varies. After shoving in the last rack of dirty dishes, I shut the machine's mammoth mouth, press its round red "start" button — and wait. Then I try everything to get it to cooperate. Eventually, it does. How long that takes is purely a matter of speculation.

I've been battling this stubborn button for three long months, ever since I began bussing tables and washing dishes in the kitchen at Princeton University's Stevenson Hall. Those of us who toil here call ourselves the "workers of the world."

Being actual workers, we're making fun of the rich-kid "Marxists" on campus who parrot the Communist manifesto: "Workers of the world, unite! You have nothing to lose but your chains!" These so-called revolutionaries know nothing of the real "workers of the world" who labor in the back end of Stevenson's kitchen.

As a scholarship kid, I have no "chains" to break. Six nights a week, I cheerfully tie a white plastic apron over my worn corduroys and tattered Princeton sweatshirt. I'm happy to swap the grind of

1

studying for a few hours in the kitchen, where I can lose myself in the mundane motions of scraping, wiping and spraying plates.

I'm thankful to have this steady job. It covers my books and everyday expenses — and it has introduced me to fine, real-world men like Cleveland "Cleve" Washington, an expert cook, and John "Caddie" Cahill, who supervises the kitchen's operations.

Most nights I'm the last one in the kitchen, tackling the dishwasher alone. I always start gently, hoping it will behave. Tonight, as usual, nothing happens.

"Please!" I beg softly, as if my sweet tone might seduce the machine.

I wait, listening for the rush of water filling the tank. But no.

"Goddammit!" I bark.

Then, as usual, I resort to a harsher approach. I forcefully punch the thing.

"Oh, come *on!* Start, dammit!" Frantic by now, I bash the button again and again. "I cannot deal with this shit tonight. I need to *leave.*"

"Bruce!"

I jump backward when I hear Caddie, the big boss, shout my name. He's a tough, brawny Irishman who seems old to me — probably all of 50, I suppose. Almost military in his bearing, Caddie keeps his graying hair cropped in a crew cut. His pants are sharply creased, his white button-down shirts pristine. His entire appearance is a statement defying the counterculture uniform of most college students: long hair, colorful collarless shirts or tie-dyed t-shirts, flared bellbottom pants.

I turn to see him standing in the doorway, gazing at me with narrowed eyes. Blood rushes to my face when I realize that he heard me swearing. Even worse, I'm abusing his prized equipment.

"Caddie-" I start, before he can tell me that he won't stand for that kind of language in his kitchen. I've heard him give this speech before — not to me, but to my co-workers: the greeters and servers (who include some of the first women admitted to Princeton, just this semester), the food preparers, the humble bussers and dishwashers.

We dishwashers do our filthy, numbing work at a cramped, steamy sink, scraping countless plates of slop, using a scrub brush and, when we're rushed, our bare hands. We're the lowliest workers of *this* world. But I don't mind. The steady whir of machines, the familiar clash and clang of giant pots and cheap cutlery, all comfort me. And I love to listen to WABC's Cousin Brucie, whose Top 40 radio show booms through every shift.

"Bruce!" Caddie says again, and my stomach drops.

I never want to disappoint Caddie. In just a few months, he has taught me so much about life, in and out of the kitchen: getting the job done, being patient with machines as well as people, appreciating the value of all work.

With one step, he reaches for the radio to snap off Peter, Paul and Mary's "Leaving on a Jet Plane," underscoring what he's about to say.

* * *

I left California in the fall of 1967, two years after my father's death, still mourning and bereft. Now, a couple of years into my Ivy League education, I've realized that Caddie and Cleve, more than most of my Princeton classmates, consistently challenge my ideas and truly have changed my mind. Night after night, as I've worked alongside them, both have become father figures whom I've grown to love.

Cleve is Caddie's opposite: a 40-year-old African American who turns out hamburgers, fried chicken, mashed potatoes, and lasagna for 160 hungry Princetonians nightly. In Cleve's kitchen, I abandon myself to its homey smells: bubbling tomato sauce, chicken sizzling in hot oil, the cucumbers and onions and anchovies that he lovingly preps for his favorite project, the salad station.

To most students, Cleve is invisible, like all the cooks and janitors and librarians on campus. But he and I had hit it off right away, and he now takes care of me, slipping me a few soft white rolls during my shift to make sure I eat. He always catches my eye and winks when he hears one of the overprivileged "Marxists" advocating social change. Cleve, I've learned, has read a lot of books, and he believes that Americans need Malcolm X much more than Karl Marx.

On this night, I will begin to truly appreciate what each of these men means to me. This is the night that will bend the arc of the universe, for me and for every young man on campus. All day long, the hourly tolling of the bell in the cupola of Nassau Hall, the oldest and most revered building on campus, has taken on a baleful tone... as if it were counting down to the momentous event that will go down in history on this date: Monday, December 1, 1969.

Most nights, as I clean up the tables, students linger in the comfortable dining room, putting off their studies as they sip coffee and chain-smoke cigarettes, often snuffing out the butts in the food left on their plates instead of the ashtrays on the tables.

But tonight is different. Nobody sticks around for one more smoke. No one feels like debating whether Princeton should sever ties with a defense contractor or how the US should get out of Vietnam.

Everybody is in a hurry to leave. So am I.

This day started like every other day. I met my classmate, Ric Singer, for breakfast at Chancellor Green, the student center, at 6:45 a.m. sharp. We're always the first to arrive. By 8, we're heading to the library to study.

I share practically everything with Ric. In addition to being a good friend, he's also student administrator of Stevenson's Food Services.

Every Sunday he inquires, "What shifts do you want, Jerome?" — an inexplicable nickname he gave me shortly after we met. I quickly realized that I could pick up an open shift any day, even at the last minute. Nobody else wants extra shifts in a job that leaves you stinking and soaking wet, especially in a frigid New Jersey winter. Hair and clothing were guaranteed to freeze the minute you stepped out of the steamy, soggy kitchen.

Today, at breakfast, Ric and I talked about the kitchen schedule, the upcoming basketball season, Princeton's irascible coach. We were evading what weighed heavily on both of us — so heavily that Ric even called me by my real name. We seem to feel that if we don't mention it, maybe it won't happen.

Across the table, I watched Ric work his way through his regular breakfast. He has a funny habit of consuming each item on his tray individually, always in order: first, scrambled eggs, then bacon, and, finally, hot chocolate. Gazing out the window into the cold, dark morning, it strikes me that, tonight, Ric and I will be pitted against each other. What might that do to our friendship?

All day long, an angry murmur had blanketed the campus — a buzz you couldn't really hear, but you could definitely feel. Maybe it was detectable because, otherwise, there was nothing but eerie silence everywhere. The usual antiwar pickets and protests were absent. People were behaving almost furtively, eyes downcast, avoiding direct contact with everyone.

During my last seminar of the day, Modern American History, the entire class — including me — had struggled to pay attention to Eric Goldman's perspectives on President Lyndon Johnson's Great Society. Goldman is the main reason I'm here: after reading *Rendezvous with Destiny,* his stunning book about the history of reform movements in American politics, I had decided I needed to go to Princeton for its stellar history department.

That this had actually happened still seems like a miracle every time I attend a Goldman class. Usually he's spellbinding, but today, I noticed every single student — including me — crooking his neck every few minutes for a glance at his wristwatch.

For once, I couldn't wait to get out of Goldman's class. I'd rush through my dinner shift at Stevenson, and finally — after months of worry and anticipation — find out what my future holds.

* * *

"Bruce!" Caddie says again, and I'm dreading what he'll say next.

"I'm so sorry, Caddie – " I talk over him, hoping to preempt his speech.

"Bruce, I wanted to-"

"I... I don't have time to mess with the dishwasher tonight, Caddie. I have to leave right now." I yank my apron over my head to emphasize my point.

For a moment he stares intently at me, studying my face. Then he says quietly, "I'll get it started."

This confuses me, because Caddie is a stickler. We're always expected to finish a job, and he never does our work for us. Is he going to fire me?

He steps toward me, and, to my astonishment, throws a muscular arm around my shoulder, pulling me into a hug. I stand rigid: sweaty after a night in the kitchen, worried that I stink, utterly bewildered by his gesture.

"I wanted to say..." Caddie says softly, and I find myself leaning into him. "... I wanted to wish you the best tonight. I hope things will work out."

Tears fill my eyes. When Caddie releases me, I turn away, not wanting him to see me cry. But I can't hide the stress and worry I've buried during the day, and for so many days before.

Then he throws his arm around me again. He pulls me in, shakes me a little, and whispers into my ear, like a prayer: "Good luck!"

I chant Caddie's benediction to myself — "good luck, good luck, good luck" — with each step I take beneath the massive, skeletal maples and elms that line Prospect Avenue — The Street.

Along The Street, I first pass the old mansions that are closest to campus. No longer private homes, they now serve Princeton's wealthiest students — those who can afford the fees at these aristocratic, fraternity-like eating clubs, which offer social spaces, an activities calendar, and a specific culture in addition to meals. Stevenson, the eating club at the far end of The Street, doesn't require sophomores to "bicker" or compete for admission. The reasonable cost and policy of openness at Stevenson attract an eclectic mix of students. Environmentalists and engineers, whose buildings are nearby, share tables with jocks, lefties, many of the few women on campus, even grad students and the occasional professor.

I draw a deep breath and exhale a frosty mist. The night is clear and crisp, with just an occasional snowflake flecking the air. But the atmosphere is downright creepy. The Street is silent; no one is partying; no one is even out and about — except me. An ominous quiet blankets Princeton's Gothic buildings, its stone archways and wrought-iron fences.

Shivering, I start to sprint down The Street. The old wool overcoat I bought from a senior two years ago, when I confronted my first real winter, does little to shield me from the night's piercing cold. The fear shuddering through me only intensifies the icy tremors.

Tonight, for me and hundreds of thousands of other American men, life and death will lie in a number, to be determined by our birthdate. Tonight, in Washington, DC, a random lottery drawing will assign a number to each date of the year. That number — every young man's birthdate — will dictate the order in which we'll be drafted into military service to fight in Vietnam. The lower the number, the greater the peril.

* * *

Everyone knows the United States is losing the war in Vietnam. Protests wrack college campuses, and recruitment isn't meeting the military's growing need for manpower. To get more soldiers, the government has stepped up the draft system, which conscripts young men who lack the means to attend college. As long as they stay in school, college students are exempt. After graduation, they will be instantly eligible for the draft, and that likely means going to Vietnam. Tonight's drawing inaugurates the lottery system intended to boost enlistment while conveniently reducing opposition to the war.

President Richard Nixon's decision to institute the lottery is both cynical and politically shrewd. A lottery, on its surface, is fair; randomly and without prejudice, it distributes the responsibility to fight among all young men of draft age. However, around half the men involved in the lottery will be effectively exempt from serving because of their favorable numbers. Nixon's lottery will siphon off thousands of men who otherwise might have joined the antiwar movement out of self-interest, fearing for their own lives. This way, he can conscript more men to fight while also dousing the flames of the antiwar movement, which he despises.

This is the first time in 29 years that the United States has used a draft lottery. In the fall of 1940, a year before the United States entered World War II, some 20 million men were sorted for the military draft by birthdays, just as we'll be sorted tonight. The age range for the draft has dropped, however; today's lottery affects men between 18 and 26, while the 1940 draft lottery took in men between 21 and 36.

Ironically, most of us students aren't old enough to vote against the war. But we're old enough to die in it.

Back in 1940, to underscore the lottery's importance in defending democracy, warplanes had flown in formation over the Selective Service building while a government official solemnly stirred the 366 capsules containing birthdates (February 29 included), using a wooden paddle made from a rafter from Independence Hall. The Secretary of War, blindfolded with a swatch of fabric clipped from a chair used in the signing of the Declaration of Independence, had then handed each capsule to President Franklin D. Roosevelt, who announced its date.

Tonight, there will be no warplane flyover, no ceremonial blindfold or wooden paddle. No president or cabinet member will have the "honor" of pulling the numbers. Nixon has left that dark task to Selective Service officials. Some have refused to participate, saying they don't want to be used as props by the Nixon administration. The entire event will be conducted in full view of television cameras, so no one can cry foul.

* * *

This bizarre bingo game starts at 8 p.m. Almost every man my age will be glued to a TV or radio as our birthdays are drawn. The sooner you hear your birthday announced, the worse the news. Being among the first 120 birthdays means that you'll probably be sent to Vietnam. For college students like me, that will happen when the protection of our student deferments disappears. If my number comes up later, I'll probably be safe, free to live my life and pursue my longtime goal of going to law school and becoming a public defender.

But right now, I need a television desperately. Immediately.

Stevenson Hall isn't an option. The Trekkies control the TV room, tuning in nightly to "Star Trek" reruns. No one, nothing, interferes with their evening ritual of worshiping Captain Kirk and Mr. Spock. Not even the lottery that might upend their futures, even take their lives.

My own room in Patton Hall is out, too, because my roommates and I don't have a TV. I could sit on my bed and listen to my little AM radio, but I don't want to face this moment all by myself. Being around others who also are learning their numbers will make me feel less anxious. We can help each other cope with the news, maybe figure out what to do.

But where can I go?

Then it comes to me. The student center, over in Chancellor Green, has a TV. Lots of people will be watching there. I'll probably find somebody I know in the crowd.

As I race up the student center's steps, a guy I know from Stevenson is leaving the building. "Hey, Wasser! You here to watch 'Mayberry RFD'?" he laughs.

Of course, nobody in college ever watches "Mayberry RFD," a spin-off from "The Andy Griffith Show" that's even more countrified and mortifying than Opie. Anyway, I think CBS will preempt its usual shows to broadcast the lottery.

At the arched doorway, I peer into the hazy student center to assess the crowd for this nationally televised event. It feels like the Apollo 11 moon landing, just a few months ago. Then, Americans watched, astonished, as Neil Armstrong stepped onto the surface of the moon and proclaimed: "That's one small step for man, one giant leap for mankind."

Now, for this considerably less auspicious event, at least sixty guys are jammed into a large room already crowded with old couches, squashed pillows, and shifting, tumbling piles of trash. Everyone is facing the TV — but far from watching the 19-inch screen, they're bombarding it with any lightweight thing they can lay their hands on: wadded-up notebook pages, paper napkins, pencils, Styrofoam cups. Blue cigarette smoke hangs so dense and low over the room that I can't even see if anyone I know is here.

When a few guys sit down, I can see that the newscaster, Roger Mudd, is perched on a flimsy folding chair in some government building's frumpy old meeting room: worn brown carpet, heavy beige curtains, mismatched office furniture. Mudd, a tall man, has to twist his frame to face the camera as he speaks. I assume he's announcing each birthdate and its lottery number — but I can't hear a word.

Besides Mudd, all I can see is a somber-looking government official digging his hand, over and over, into a glass bowl holding 366 blue plastic capsules. Each capsule is a fortune cookie, its slip of paper ready to reveal every young man's fate.

Bedlam rules the room. Guys are yelling at each other, shoving anyone who blocks their view, screaming at the TV and each other: "Fuck you!" "Shut up!" "Hell no, we won't go!"

The shouting voices coalesce into an angry chant that rattles the antique light fixtures. "One! Two! Three! Four! We don't want your fucking war!"

Feet stomp and fists pound to emphasize the yelling. All around me, rage is overflowing like the ashtrays.

"Good luck!" I hear Caddie say again. I'll need it, I think, just to find out my goddamn lottery number!

I stretch my neck to see around the guys blocking my view of the black-and-white TV. I catch just a glimpse of a jaunty holiday commercial for Norelco shavers.

"Sit down! We can't see!" someone in back yells to the guys in front.

"Fuck off!" someone in front yells back.

When a few people finally sit down and I get a clearer view of the screen, I see that the camera is showing only a few rows of dates at a time, not the whole board. I don't see my birthday.

Frustrated, I walk back out to the lobby, where a guy I don't know is sitting on a folding chair, cradling a transistor radio to his ear. His foot and knee are bouncing rapidly, like a jackhammer.

"Hey," I call out, "you find out anything?"

"This is bullshit," he says, his leg still jiggling. "It's impossible! The announcer is calling out birthdays and numbers so fast that I can't tell if a birthday goes with the number before or after the date."

He doesn't look at me when he talks. He seems to be simply registering his exasperation with the universe.

"They called my birthday," he continues, "but I still don't know my fucking number! I'm either 91 or 347."

"Maybe *The Daily Prince* will publish the list tomorrow," I say — and it gives me an idea. I can go to *The Prince's* office to see if the editors have the list. They've got to have a Teletype machine!

But where the hell is the campus newspaper office? I have no idea.

Then I remember that there's a teletype machine outside of WPRB-FM, the campus radio station, in the basement of Holder Hall. When I lived in Holder last year, I always checked the scores of the Boston Celtics games there. That machine has to be spitting out lottery numbers.

* * *

I rush back out into the frigid night air, needing only a few minutes to cover the short distance from Chancellor Green to Holder Hall. As soon as I see the Gothic building, my mind is flooded with memories of last year's juvenile antics. As a sophomore, I'd shared a suite in Holder with a high school friend, Chris Lipsett, and another guy. We were way up in a corner turret of the U-shaped dorm, only steps away from Commons.

I had earned the reputation of being what Princetonians called a "flamer" — short for a flaming asshole. This meant that I shamelessly involved myself in frequent inane stunts. For example, during the first snowfall of my sophomore year — before women were admitted — I happily participated in the nude Winter Olympics held in the Holder quadrangle. Events included jumping jacks, push-ups, and relay races — all by participants wearing only smiles.

At Princeton, exams were not proctored, offering rich opportunities for flamers to compete in outrageousness. During the final in my freshman sociology course, ten upperclassmen lined up on a narrow balcony that framed the classroom and mooned dozens of shocked test-takers. Another flamer disrupted a final simply by snapping his fingers — summoning into the classroom a scantily clad woman carrying a waiter's tray bearing half-filled wine glasses.

I became known for my own unique prank in my freshman dorm, Witherspoon Hall. Built in the 1870s, the building was heated with big, bulky, clanking radiators. These relics from the previous century absolutely fascinated me. Coming from San Diego, I had never seen anything like them.

One evening, I pocketed some of the half-eaten fruit left on plates at the Commons and returned to "'Spoon" with a plan. I lodged the apples and oranges in the bowels of the downstairs radiator. Soon

15

enough, pungent odors wafted through the dorm. This instant success led me to repeat the prank.

Imitators seized upon this stunt, provoking the ire of Stanley, the janitor. Invariably, I caught the blame. Stanley would corner me as I walked to class and threaten me.

"Wasser," he'd say, not even half-smiling, "if I catch you stuffing that shit in the radiators again, I'm gonna make you lick it out with your tongue!"

I would look him straight on. With my best poker face, I would innocently reply, "Stan, what are you talking about? I'd never do such a thing!"

* * *

All that seems so long ago now.

As I walk downstairs to the radio station, I see two guys who must have just found out their numbers. I don't have to ask. They climb the stairs without a word. One hangs back, as if his shoes are full of cement, laboring on each step. The other bounds up lightly, taking the steps two at a time.

The familiar rat-a-tat of the teletype calls to me. On the table, thick pleats of white perforated paper spill into receiving trays. Usually the pages stack onto themselves, folding neatly into an accordion. But tonight, some are ripped apart and strewn around, with one pile cascading to the floor. Clearly, others have checked here before me.

I rifle through the crumpled sheets, but I can't think straight, can't find what I'm looking for. "Slow down," I say to myself. Then, out loud: "Look for a list."

But the machine's annoying clickety-clack and constant spewing of paper amps up my agitation. The sheer volume of news stories the machine transmits seems to mock the one story, the single number, that I seek. Now my quest feels insignificant and strangely irrelevant.

"But the lottery is the only thing that matters to me tonight," I hear myself say, making my case to the machine, as if it were alive.

I take a deep breath and start again, scanning the evening's news stories:

- Los Angeles Police Chief Edward Davis announced arrest warrants for members of the Manson cult on murder charges.
- The first legislation to limit aircraft noise levels at airports was introduced into the US Federal Air Regulations.
- The first peacetime draft lottery in the United States since 1940 was held. September 14 was the first of the 366 days of the year selected.

Peacetime? Now is *peacetime?* That's bullshit! It's Orwellian! Just a few days ago, what they call "the My Lai massacre" was in all the papers, all over the radio and TV. A year ago, in a little Vietnamese village, American soldiers brutally murdered some 500 people — women, children, old people. The military kept the whole horrifying story secret until an investigative reporter uncovered the facts.

Then I reread the last headline, and relief sweeps over me. September 14. Right on! At least I'm not Number One!

Slowing down, I neatly fold page after page as I search for the list itself. I come upon a sports story about the Celts, but I don't even stop to read it. Instead, I force myself to keep running through pages, looking for one that has lots of numbers in a sea of white.

Maybe, I think, whoever got here before me tore off all the pages and took the whole list. Then what do I do? I guess I'll have to stand here and wait for the Associated Press to retransmit it. How long will that take?

But then — just as my panic surges — my eyes fall on what I'm looking for. Not only has the AP printed the complete draft lottery list; it also has conveniently organized the numbers according to the calendar.

Breathless, I scour the sheets. January. February. March. April.

I run my index finger down, just past the first two weeks of the month: 13, 14, 15, 16, 17.

I land on April 18.

I slide my finger along an invisible line to the right-hand column. It comes to rest beneath two numerals.

My heart pounds in my ears. I stop breathing.

There it is. The answer to my question. My draft number.

90.

I am 90.

As I stumble out of Holder Hall, back into the dark night, I feel dazed. Blinking away tears, I wonder which way to go.

I don't want to head back to the dorm and talk lottery numbers with my roommates. We aren't especially close, and the last thing I need is a couple of near-strangers who might be celebrating the good fortune of their safe numbers.

The wind has picked up, and the temperature seems to have dropped another ten degrees. I pull up the collar of my wool coat and yank down my black-and-orange Princeton knitted hat to withstand the bitter cold.

As I inhale and exhale the biting air, I feel weirdly alive. Stars shimmer like jewels against the black velvet sky. I have a profound sense of loneliness and, at the same time, a deep feeling of connection to the world and events around me.

I decide to walk for a while. Maybe the cold air will help me gain some clarity.

But, before I left the teletype machine, I couldn't help looking up two more lottery numbers: the days before and after my birthday. April 17 was 260. April 19 was 336.

Why couldn't I have been born one day earlier or one day later? Either one would have placed me far from military service and given me a green light to my future.

Then I hear my dad's voice in my mind, loud and clear. "Son," he's asking, "if you 'if' in one hand and shit in the other, which hand gets fuller?" Dad never hesitated to remind me of how foolish it was to speculate about hypothetical or alternate possibilities.

The truth is that April 18th is part of my identity. I had always liked sharing my birthday with Paul Revere's midnight ride, in 1775, with his famous warning to the colonial militia: "The British are coming!" April 18 is also the day when, in 1906, an earthquake and subsequent fire destroyed much of San Francisco. It's the day Albert Einstein died.

I was born in 1949, during Passover, a holiday of deliverance and a celebration of the Jews' escape from slavery in ancient Egypt. Even now, the first night of Passover is when all the world's Jews still ask the same question: Why is this night different from all other nights?

Tonight, my birthday makes this night different.

Until now, I had no personal connection to the war in Vietnam. But tonight, suddenly, I've lost the luxury of seeing the war as a distant abstraction. The draft lottery has made it frighteningly real.

All because of my birthday! A joyous annual celebration — with family and friends, cake and candles and applause, for the past twenty years — suddenly has transformed into a life sentence. Or maybe a death sentence.

I'll never feel the same way about April 18th again.

* * *

I am 90.

Walking through the night, surprisingly, I'm not quite as cold as I was earlier.

Actually, I'm thinking, this terrible lottery number shouldn't come as a surprise. I've always had what I called "Wasser luck" — no luck at all. Anything that involves chance is likely to result in the worst possible outcome. When I turned 16 and took my driver's license test, I was assigned the examiner with the most brutal reputation. Of course, I flunked. Two days before I was scheduled to take my SAT, my appendix burst. On my way to my first date with Maryanne Callery, the high-school homecoming queen, I got a flat tire and had no way to contact her.

Did I really think the universe would smile upon me now?

During those high-school disasters, I'd missed my dad something awful, even though I generally knew what he'd say. He would tell me to "shake it off," in his soft Southern accent. I knew he meant I needed to work harder to overcome adversity.

But this — this wasn't about working harder. This random blow isn't something I can "shake off" or work harder to resolve.

My dad had always known how to comfort and guide me in practically any situation. But I've noticed lately that, with each passing day, his voice has diminished a little in my memory. I have to work harder to hear him, to imagine what he would say.

January 28, 1965. Just about four years now. He had battled cancer for 18 months, during my first two years of high school. When Dad died, our family was shattered. I — the eldest child and only boy — withdrew from my two younger sisters and our heartbroken mother.

Throwing myself into school, I vowed that my performance would bring honor to the man I loved so fiercely. But no matter what I did, deep down I knew this loss had gutted me.

To fill the void, I sought replacements. My high-school basketball coach, Dick Eiler, was my first surrogate father. I'm sure pity and compassion drove him to find a place for me on the team.

There were other substitutes, too, but none as important as my heroes and imaginary fathers, Dr. Martin Luther King, Jr., and Robert F. Kennedy. Both men were young, like my dad; they were charismatic, and they stood for something greater than themselves. Their crushing deaths, just weeks apart in that awful spring of 1968, compounded my losses.

A year before they were killed, I had turned 18 and duly registered with the Selective Service System, requesting a routine student deferment. I didn't think much about what any of it meant.

Bobby's murder, right after King's, changed everything. These brutal assassinations not only plunged me into a deeper grief; they convinced me that I could not bear any more violence. And I absolutely could not, ever, kill anyone.

The following morning, I notified my draft board that I was applying for conscientious-objector status.

At the time, there was no real need to make this decision, and I'd heard nothing at all about my request. I knew, though, that my chances of being granted CO status were extremely low — especially with my local draft board being in San Diego, a notoriously conservative, pro-military city.

What would happen if my CO request was denied? I'd refuse to report for induction. That meant that I would be arrested, charged with a felony, tried and probably convicted. I would go to prison. After serving my sentence, as a convicted felon, I wouldn't be allowed to vote. And I would never realize my dream of becoming a criminal public defender. No state bar association would ever consider admitting me.

I had always wanted to be a dedicated servant to my country. But my revulsion at the thought of bearing arms outweighed everything.

Now, with a brand-new urgency, one burning question after another races through my mind: How can I act on my beliefs without ruining my life? If I don't fight, what kind of American am I? What kind of *man* am I?

I recall the contempt back in San Diego toward men who refused to fight: the ugly taunts, the frequent homophobic slurs. What would my dad, who had served in World War II, have thought of me? How would my new reality affect my mother, who had already lost so much? What about my next year and a half at Princeton? What would Cleve and Caddie think of me? Will they think I'm a coward?

Then I remember the men who didn't have my choice, those who were already fighting and dying in a war I repudiated. I had learned that, during the Civil War, wealthy men could "buy" a substitute to serve in their place. Was I no different from them by continuing to go to Princeton?

Fear and shame shudder through me. How could I look a veteran in the eye? How could I face my Stevenson Hall friend Ray Butler, who had already served in Vietnam?

I'm not the flag-waving type, but I have an abiding love for the United States. This is the place that welcomed Grandma Rose Plotkin from Russia, and Grandpa Ben Berliner from Poland. Here, there was no persecution, no pogroms — only possibilities. Now, am I turning my back on a country that gave my relatives everything?

Others in my family had avoided military service. In fact, it was Bismarck's "Blood and Iron" forced conscription in 1860s Germany that drove my great-grandfather, Abram "Buppa" Wasser, to faraway America. And Uncle Abe Plotkin had fled Czarist Russia in 1915 with his sister, my Grandma Rose, to escape compulsory service.

But some of my relatives *had* served in the military, and I was raised to respect and honor those who wore the uniform. My Uncle Allan served in World War I, although he was immediately captured by the Germans and spent most of the war as a POW. Even Uncle Abe, after refusing to fight for the Czar, enlisted as a US soldier in World War II.

My father, an Army man, spent the war stationed at Fort Lewis, in the state of Washington. He so impressed the officers that, after World War II ended, they offered him a civilian post at Fort Lawton in Seattle. While Dad wasn't one to talk much about his wartime days, he kept his Army dress jacket, clean and pressed, in his office closet.

But Vietnam — this is nothing like the Second World War. Vietnam isn't a menace to my country. Over there, far from fighting for freedom, I would be caught up in a vicious, long-running civil war that other countries' meddling has inflated to international significance. Unlike Dad, I wouldn't be fighting for humanity. I don't really know what I *would* be fighting for.

My head swirls in confusion.

* * *

As I walk along the path, four drunk guys stagger past me. No hats, no gloves; their jackets aren't even zipped. They must've just come from a bar on Nassau Street. Hanging on each other, they loudly slur-sing: "O Canada! We stand on guard for thee. O Canada! We stand on guard for *THEEEEEEE!*"

Canada? Had they learned the Canadian national anthem from watching hockey games? Are they thinking about fleeing to Canada?

That had never even occurred to me as an option. I can't leave the United States. If I left the country, I'd surrender my chance to influence social change. My studies have already taught me that African Americans, despite centuries of wrong, never gave up on America. I can't, either; I'd rather go to jail. A conscientious objector never rejects his obligation to his country. I would be required to serve in some capacity — just not as a soldier.

24

As this thought takes shape, a blast of rock music explodes from open windows in the dorms above me, piercing the quiet of the night. Raucous shouts — "Fuck the war!" "I'm free... I'm free!" "Yeah, baby!" — rain down upon me. I look up, realizing that many of my classmates are celebrating their lucky numbers. I feel happy for them, genuinely pleased that their lives are spared and their futures some-what assured.

At the same time, I'm reminded of something I've seen all too often here: Princeton, for all its eminent intellectual attainments, fails to produce empathetic, compassionate people. Reasonably sensitive men would realize that this is not a night for open celebration; sober reflection and sympathy for the less fortunate would have been far more appropriate. Once again, I sense that I don't belong in this bastion of privilege, where wealth and power so seamlessly drape their invisible protection over the well-born.

I head away from the fabled residential halls, stung again by shame that I chose such a place to get an education. Even more off-putting is the realization that these affluent students will always be able to distance themselves from people destined to bear the burden of their good fortune. Our life trajectories — theirs and mine — will never truly intersect. I sit next to these men every day, in every class, but I will never again see them as my classmates.

Loneliness sweeps over me.

Then I think of Jim. Jim Lieber.

* * *

Jim and I met during the spring semester of our sophomore year. We were taking one of Princeton's most storied under-graduate classes, Constitutional Interpretation, and I was in way over my head.

25

Jim was one of the few other sophomores, so at first we shared a certain intimidation. As we got to know each other, we were struck by our similarities: both six feet tall, strong, athletically inclined, with dark curly hair and flashing brown eyes. We were alike in other ways, too, from sharing a great love of basketball and baseball, to being reform Jews with a messianic vision of making the world a better place. It wasn't long before we realized we could be brothers.

But there were differences, of course, and all of them left me wishing I could be more like him. I couldn't hope to approach Jim's eloquence. When he spoke, it sounded as if he were reading from a gracefully crafted script — though, invariably, it was utterly spontaneous. Like me, Jim was a political rarity at Princeton in his support for Bobby Kennedy, whose passionate commitment to ending both the war in Vietnam and inequality in America made him something of a pariah among Princeton's urbane, sophisticated fans of Eugene McCarthy.

Until I met Jim, I had felt like a complete imposter at Princeton. I was terribly insecure and bewildered, convinced that Admissions must have made a colossal mistake by accepting me. When I applied, I had no idea what this place would be like. I didn't realize Princeton prided itself on being the "southernmost northern university" in the country. All I knew was that it was an Ivy League school, and, to me, that meant the best in the nation.

What I also didn't know was that many of the 800 students in my class had attended Andover, Exeter, or some other swanky prep school back east. The well-off "swells" repulsed me; their rooms, from my occasional glance, seemed to scream wealth, from their fancy stereos and expensive TVs to their cut crystal cocktail glasses and elaborate steins for imported beer. I was constantly asking myself, "What the fuck am I doing here?"

Even though my grades were fine, I never got over the feeling that I wasn't as good as everyone else. I was desperately poor by Princeton standards; I couldn't even afford the impulsive purchase of a ten-cent candy bar. I didn't drink; I didn't smoke; I didn't do dope. Couldn't afford any of that.

It felt like a big "L" was tattooed on my forehead — for "loser" — just like Hester Prynne's scarlet letter. So it's not surprising that I deeply cherished my friendship with Jim, though I often wondered what he saw in me. When I asked him, he said he valued my interesting contributions in discussions, my compassion, and my drive for learning. But he said what he loved most was that I could always make him laugh.

Around Jim, for the first time since I'd arrived at Princeton, I felt I could be myself. As I got to know him better, I recognized in him a maturity far beyond his years. I came to view him as a kind of *tzedek* — a wise, highly learned Jewish spiritual master.

Where is he tonight? I wonder. What's his lottery number? I was so rattled at the teletype machine that I hadn't thought to look it up. His birthday – April 14th — is just a few days before mine. Then I think: *I hope he's not in the same mess I'm in. I hope he won the draft lottery tonight.*

And with that thought, I know where to go. Picking up my pace, I run toward Jim's dorm. As my heart races, I generate a cloud of steam, surrounding myself with my own breath. The walk from Henry Hall usually takes about seven minutes, but I make it in four.

A blast of warm air slugs me as I push through his dorm's front door. I hadn't realized until this moment how cold I've been, and the heat immediately makes my hands and feet tingle.

Stairs up, two by two, up to his floor, down the hall to his suite. He shares it with three other guys, none of whom I know.

I pound on the door. Some guy with long, wavy brown hair, dressed in sweatpants and the standard Princeton sweatshirt, opens the door.

"Hey, is Jim here?" I ask. I can hear the despair and desperation in my voice.

"No."

My whole body slumps in disappointment. "Do you know when he'll be back?" I ask, grasping for hope.

"No, but I wouldn't wait around if I were you."

"Oh! Why not?"

"Don't think he'll be up to talking when he gets in," the roommate snorts. "He went to Nassau Street to get shit-faced."

"Shit-faced?" My eyebrows shoot up. To my knowledge, Jim rarely drinks.

"Someone told him his lottery number," the roommate says matter-of-factly. From his tone, it's clear this guy got a safe lottery number.

Already, I'm learning to identify a man's draft risk simply by observing his body language. In fact, tonight really *has* changed everything. From now on, when any man my age meets another, the first question will be: "What's your number?" And the second, if necessary, will be: "What are you going to do about it?"

Then the roommate adds off-handedly, "Jim's number is 31."

Tuesday, December 2, 1969

At breakfast the next morning, my downcast eyes and slumped posture tell Ric all he needs to know about my number. Still, I try to hide my gnawed cuticles and bitten fingernails from him. This bad habit always gives me away, revealing my anxiety and self-doubt.

Right now, predictably, my hands are a mess. Before leaving my room, I'd upbraided myself. "How the hell am I going to convince a draft board that I'm sincere and resolute if I don't even have the discipline to stop biting my nails?"

I glance down at Ric's hands. His fingernails are handsomely trimmed, a contrast that only feeds the self-conscious shame of my red, raw cuticles. I envy him for his self-control.

Or maybe he simply got a decent number. From his posture, I suspect he is safe, but his quiet demeanor makes me wonder.

"So what did you draw last night, Sheldon?" I don't know how I came up with that nickname for him, any more than I know why he calls me Jerome. I'm the only one who uses it, and right now I'm trying to sound casual, like we're talking about the cards in last week's game of Hearts. But I see that Ric is agitated, shifting uncomfortably in his chair.

"I got lucky, Jerome," he says, without much enthusiasm.

"How lucky?"

"VERY lucky!" he says, obviously not wanting to share his exact, enviable number with me.

"I'm happy for you, Ric —"

"But," he cuts me off, "I don't feel all that good about it."

"It's okay. I'm glad for —"

"It's hard to feel good when, you know, you're worried about your friends."

"It's all right," I say quietly. "I'm happy for you. You shouldn't see your good luck as responsible for my bad number."

"But in some ways, that's exactly what a lottery is." Ric narrows his eyes, focusing on his thoughts. "Someone else pays the price for the guy who's 'lucky.' The way I see it, Bruce... I get to go to law school, like I always planned, and you don't."

"You feel guilty?"

"Yeah, wouldn't you?"

"I don't know, Ric. But I know *you* didn't do anything wrong. Neither did I." In trying to comfort him, I'm also trying to reassure myself.

"Look, Ric, be rational. You aren't being rewarded in some weird cosmic way for being good, and I'm not being punished for being bad."

I stop talking, looking down at my half-eaten breakfast, then at my bitten nails. I know the first part of that sentence is true, but — rational or not — I believe I drew 90 because I did something wrong.

In my heart, I wonder if my lottery number *is* punishment for some awful transgression. Did I let Dad down when he was dying? Was I wrong to leave my family for Princeton when we were still mourning his death? Was this divine retribution for not being willing to serve in the military?

30

* * *

After breakfast, as I trudge toward the library, my thoughts veer sharply to Jim. I imagine he's hung over after last night. Worse, he's in even greater peril than I am. Maybe we can sort this out together. Make some kind of plan for the future. When we get past all this, maybe we can fulfill my dream of establishing a law practice together.

I figure I'll find Jim at the library, where I plan to spend the day preparing for Professor Garvey's "American Political Thought" lecture, but I don't see him as I walk into the large main reading room. Spotting an empty space at one of the old wooden desks, I spread out my books and papers to work on my draft of the "minute" — a one-page distillation of this week's required reading — to submit this evening.

Garvey, a graduate of the Air Force Academy, brings masculine toughness as well as the idealism of the 1960s to his demanding classes. He is an inflexible drill sergeant with his writing students, insisting that we be brief and precise to achieve what he calls "literary virility." Like any drill instructor, he barks orders to his students: "Make it march!" "Lean it and clean it!" "Use Anglo-Saxon words instead of Latin. Say 'shit' instead of 'defecate.'" "Ask yourself: 'If so, what next?' After *each sentence.*"

Like any DI, Garvey is in your face. He will break us down and remake us in the image of the writers he admires: Hemingway, Steinbeck, Faulkner.

For "American Political Thought," he grades our "minutes" on a rubric consisting of five elements: research, content, conciseness, style, and grammar. A 1 is the top grade, a 5 the lowest. My "minutes" have never made it past a 2, and I have little hope for the paper due tonight.

31

The theme is interdependence: the idea that we are all interconnected, and our individual choices have social consequences — an extremely relevant topic, given the lottery and my conversation with Ric this morning. But I don't see how I can squeeze my personal dilemma into a one-page essay. Consequently, my words do not "march"; instead, they meander. My argument feels vague, unfocused. My paper looks as bleak as my future.

I am awe-struck and intimidated by Gerald Garvey. He personifies intellectual rigor and carries himself with an almost regal bearing. Although he's barely six feet tall, he seems to tower over us. Beneath a receding hairline, his fair-skinned oval face features blond eyebrows over striking pale-green eyes. On campus, I never see him in anything but a three-piece suit.

Garvey is among the elite whom David Halberstam would later call "the best and brightest." These "whiz kids" — leaders in industry and academia whom President John F. Kennedy brought into his administration — crafted a foreign policy that Halberstam characterized as "brilliant," yet defying "common sense." Ultimately, their policies led to hubristic arrogance, the folly of the Vietnam war, and other misguided attempts to remake the world in America's image.

Garvey, I knew, had gone to Washington, DC, as a defense policy analyst; there, he had dedicated himself to President John F. Kennedy's "New Frontier," helping to create modern, forward-looking domestic and foreign policies under the leadership of the first president born in the 20th century.

Kennedy's 1961 inaugural address was a call to action that achieved instant fame: "Let every nation know, whether it wishes us well or ill, that we shall pay any price, bear any burden, meet any hardship, support any friend, oppose any foe, in order to assure the survival and the success of liberty...

"And so, my fellow Americans: ask not what your country can do for you — ask what you can do for your country."

Back at Princeton, Garvey held his students to the same standard of commitment. He saw his class as our own New Frontier.

* * *

In an unexpected turn of events, I had come to know Garvey and his family personally. At a Princeton baseball game the previous spring, I'd noticed my "Constitutional Interpretation" professor sitting with his wife, daughter and three sons in the bleachers. Garvey was deeply involved in the game, but his kids seemed bored, and his wife looked harried as she dug into a bottomless canvas bag, stuffed with coloring books and toys to keep them occupied.

At Princeton, I felt terribly isolated. College campuses generally are bubbles, divorced from everyday life, insulated from children and the elderly. I felt desperate to be with little kids. So I took a deep breath and mustered up my courage.

"Hi," I said, as I approached the family. "I'm Bruce Wasser, one of your students." I looked at my professor, and then turned to his wife. "Would you mind... May I take your kids for a walk?"

Happily surprised, Garvey's wife didn't seem to know what to say. I'm sure none of her husband's students, who idolized the man, had ever asked to spend time with their children. Then gratitude took over, and Mrs. Garvey introduced herself to me as Lou Ann.

"How kind of you!" she said, sizing me up. "Gerry and I don't get much of a chance to be by ourselves." Gerry! I would never think to call her husband anything but Professor Garvey, and it had never occurred to me that anyone else would either — even his wife.

"Go ahead and take them... maybe get some ice cream somewhere." She opened her purse to pay for the treat, but I refused her money.

For the next hour, the kids and I wandered around campus. Over at Commons, we even found a kind student administrator who served us ice cream cones. When we returned to the game, the youngest boy ran up to his mother. "Mommy, Mommy, can Bruce come to our house and play?"

That's how I became a fixture in the Garveys' living room on Sunday evenings, while my professor and his wife went out on a date. During these visits, I came to know Lou Ann, who was not only beautiful and unfailingly pleasant, but also every bit her husband's intellectual equal. I loved their children and looked forward to watching "The Wonderful World of Disney" with them before tucking them into bed. At the end of the evening, Professor Garvey always discreetly slipped me a couple of bucks, even though I didn't expect a cent for the happy hours I spent with his children.

Those Sunday evenings offered me a treasured opportunity to experience family life again, and to become closer to a man who could be another father figure. I eagerly shared my feelings with him in his home, but he remained remote and unemotional. I needed him as a professor, a role model, a father, but he didn't seem to need me.

Maybe we were, as Garvey believed, interdependent — but not emotionally connected.

* * *

Gathering my papers and books, I realize that I've holed myself up in the library all day long. Hustling to make Garvey's class on time, I notice yesterday's foreboding atmosphere lingers. Men are eyeing one another suspiciously, wondering: What is *his lottery* number?

I recall the day after Martin Luther King's murder, in the spring of my freshman year. Fear and suspicion had permeated the campus. Much like today, a smoldering, simmering anger was palpable as students — all of us shaken by events — focused only on where they were going, careful to avoid looking at each other. I remember how

Black students glared at white students, probably thinking: Who are you, really? Can you be trusted? Are *you* a racist?

Garvey lectures in a modern, banked classroom in the prestigious Woodrow Wilson School, a highly selective academic department that accepts only the best and brightest undergraduates to study in a program combining politics, history, economics, and world affairs. Jim is one of Wilson's shining lights; I never even applied. Though we usually walk to Garvey's class together, he isn't at our usual meeting spot, so I continue a fast walk to get to class on time.

I take my usual seat in the front row, to Garvey's right, where I can look up from my furious note-taking to watch the man in action. At 6:59, one minute before class begins, he enters the lecture hall, arms weighed down with a dozen books. For the next two and a half hours, he will speak as he always does, without notes, on the topic of the evening, pausing only to quote from one of his hardcover tomes. In a dramatic voice that alternates between a thunderous roar and a barely audible whisper, Garvey launches into his lecture on "The Declaration of Interdependence," exploring how we are connected in unintended and invisible ways to each other and the world.

Before entering Princeton, I had splurged on a Cross ballpoint pen for $5.95 — one of the extremely rare extravagances I allowed myself. By now, my tight grip had worn away the fine silver filigree of the pen's shaft. Tonight, as usual, I can't keep up with Garvey, my note-taking woefully behind his tightly constructed arguments.

During his lectures, Garvey and I have developed a kind of symbiosis. Every five minutes or so, he looks over at me and drills into me with his eyes, inaudibly asking if I'm keeping up. I nod and smile to acknowledge him — even though I'm often way behind.

Tonight, as Garvey reads a section of Dr. Martin Luther King's 1967 Christmas sermon on peace. "All life is interrelated!" Garvey emphatically gestures as he reads from Dr. King's sermon. "We are all caught in an inescapable network of mutuality, tied into a single garment of destiny."

Listening eagerly, I remember that, during one of our Sunday evening talks, I had told Garvey how much I admired King. I even admitted that the slain Nobel Peace Prize winner had served as an imaginary surrogate father to me. Now, strangely, I realize that Garvey has stopped glancing over at me — a significant, unsettling alteration in his speaking style.

"Whatever affects one directly, affects all indirectly." I set down my pen and stop taking notes. Narrowing my eyes, I try to figure out what's happening here. It's starting to feel... *personal*. Even though he isn't looking at me, I know he's speaking directly to me since I've told him I'm against the war. Is Garvey reprimanding me for refusing to support and serve in his New Frontier?

The truth of King's words is searing. As Garvey speaks, I realize that the deaths of American men in Vietnam are part of this "garment of destiny." My privilege of sitting comfortably in the Woodrow Wilson School comes at a cost to others, those victimized by poverty and racism, who bear the brunt of this terrible war.

I turn around in my chair to catch Jim's attention; he is seated back in the last row. His number makes him even more vulnerable than I am. I stare, but I can't tell what he's thinking. Is he hearing this? Taking it as personally as I am? He keeps his eyes locked on Garvey, and, to my surprise, never looks back at me. That familiar feeling of loneliness shivers through me.

"We are made to live together because of the interrelated structure of reality..., " I shift my gaze back to Garvey. "This is the way our universe is structured; this is its interrelated quality."

Suddenly, I feel my face flush with humiliation. Now I get it: Garvey has singled me out, and, cleverly, he is using my idol's words against me. He is quoting King to indict my choice not to serve, my student deferment, my abandonment of honorable decision-making.

Both Garvey and King are shaking a finger at me for my moral failings. I'm sure of it.

I swallow hard, working not to break down.

As Garvey launches into his summarizing peroration — "Each person's actions influences the actions of others" — a sense of relief ripples through me. This public/private shaming is finally coming to a close.

I gather my books quickly, without a glance at the man who has cast aspersions on me, and bolt out of the classroom.

In the foyer, I scan the crowd, frantically looking for Jim. There he is, standing near the window, digging into his flapped, black briefcase. He must be waiting for me.

"Jim!" I call out, but he doesn't hear me. "Jim!" I push past other students in the crowd to find a path to him.

"Bruce!" When he finally spots me, I'm startled to see that his face is pasty white, his eyes heavily lidded, as he booms out my name.

"Jim – I heard about your number. I... I'm so sorry —"

He cuts me off. "You heard wrong!" His eyebrows rise, his eyes widen. "So did I!"

"What? What do you mean?"

"My number is 231, *not* 31!"

"231! Really!" I'm shocked. "That's great!"

"Yeah, what a crazy roller coaster last night!" He shakes his head, as if to clear it.

"What happened?"

"In all the chaos, my roommate thought he heard my number was 31. And that's what he told me. I believed him. I was so devastated that I went to Nassau Inn to get plastered. I never do that, and boy, did I ever pay for it this morning! Barely could get here tonight."

"231! Jim, that's fantastic. You —"

"I'll tell you what's fantastic." He cuts me off. "Now, I can drop out of 'Orgo.'" "Orgo" is Princeton's notoriously difficult organic chemistry class, a prerequisite for pre-med students that weeds out many hopefuls.

"In fact," Jim continues, "I don't need to take *any* more pre-med classes."

"Wait! Orgo! What are you talking about, Jim? I thought you wanted to be a lawyer?"

"Yeah, but I was taking the prerequisites so I could apply to medical school. That was my insurance policy, to get out of going to Vietnam. You know that med students can keep their student deferments. But I wasn't ever really interested in medicine!"

"Oh! I'm so happy for you. That's great! Now you can do what you love — become a lawyer... and a writer. Do all the things you've dreamed of!"

Then, Jim gets quiet and stares intently at me. I suspect he's worrying about what my number might be and whether my future is imperiled. Finally, he asks tentatively, "What was your draw?"

Still getting accustomed to my new identity, I stumble when I say, "I... I'm 90."

"Oh, damn!" Jim's abnormally pale, but now he's alert with genuine concern. "Damn! Damn! I'm so sorry!"

"Yeah. I don't know what to do."

"But now everything makes sense," Jim turns thoughtful. "Now I see what was happening in Garvey's class."

We're outside now, walking toward the upper campus together; Jim is unusually quiet, clearly running something through his head. I've seen him do this before when he's considering every angle of an argument.

Finally, he stops abruptly, grabs my elbow and looks directly at me. "I saw how upset you were."

"Yeah," I look away, embarrassed by my open emotion. "That was awful!"

"You thought Garvey was talking directly to you, didn't you? You thought he was indicting you?"

"It felt personal!" My stomach churns again; nausea swirls in my throat. "He wouldn't even look at me, and he *always* makes eye contact. I felt ... judged."

"He was too wrapped up in what he was saying to look at anyone," Jim says. "His eyes were darting all over the place."

"I try so hard to do well in his course, Jim." Now I'm confessing my deepest frustrations. "But I never seem to be able to please him."

"You weren't his intended audience! Don't you see, Bruce? Garvey was aiming at the guys you can't stand! You know, the 'gentlemen' — the snobs in Ivy and Cottage. He was basically saying they are selfish and greedy and indifferent to the world around them."

"Maybe... or maybe he was saying that to me. He knows how I feel about the war."

Jim shakes his head. "For all we know, that whole lecture wasn't about any of us."

"What do you mean?"

"This could be all about *him* and *his* work under JFK, making God knows what policy that led to this horrible war in Vietnam."

Now, I see what Jim is thinking; he chooses his words carefully as he explains.

"It could be that he blames himself for creating and contributing to this mess, and now he sees that it landed on *us* — his cherished students. He never thought he would know — and even love — the young men who might pay the price for the fantasies of their New Frontier. Maybe he couldn't look at any of us out of his *own* guilt and shame. Our blood will be on his hands."

Maybe Jim's right. That would explain my limited relationship with Garvey. No matter how much time I spend with him, no matter how much I do for him, he never lets down his guard, never lets me grow close to him. I feel his affection, but he doesn't allow the relationship to deepen.

"The way I see it, that whole lecture was an admission of the consequences of his actions while serving in the Kennedy administration." Jim lays out his theory as if he's already a lawyer, making his all-important closing argument.

"Maybe it was an apology for how he knows it will alter our lives." Jim's dark eyes burn as he emphasizes his point. "*He* probably feels judged by *us!*"

"Maybe," I say, thinking through what Jim has figured out. He always seems to know just what to say, to change the way I look at things. "I hadn't thought of that. It makes me feel a little better."

But then, I flash on Garvey's cold delivery of "The Declaration of Interdependence." Shame shudders through me again as I recall his vivid gesturing before the class, his sudden avoidance of my gaze. I hear him bellow his blistering words: "We are all tied in a single garment of destiny!"

"I'm not so sure, Jim." My guilt, self-doubt and general misery won't be soothed so fast. "I hope you're right," I add quickly, "but I just don't know."

SUNDAY, DECEMBER 21, 1969
WINTER BREAK, JUNIOR YEAR

"Mom, I need to talk to you."

Taking a deep breath, I face the morning, back home in San Diego for winter break.

Having already made coffee, Mom is now aggressively sponging away any stray grounds — though I don't see even a speck.

Emotionally depleted after the past semester, I immediately relaxed into the soothing, perpetually mild climate of Southern California. New Jersey's biting winds and the crushing events of the past month had conspired to chill my spirits; now, I'm eager to see the ocean, to hear the Pacific rhythmically lapping onto San Diego's beaches.

I also know that, beach or no beach, this winter break won't be any kind of vacation. It's time to tell my mother what my lottery number means: that I intend to officially pursue conscientious objection.

With dread, I take Mom's arm, tentatively, at her elbow. I need her to stop attacking the spotless counter and, instead, sit down with me at our shiny, chrome-framed kitchen table.

I pull out her chair, brightly covered in yellow vinyl, and gently steer her onto the seat. Then I sit down opposite her.

"... And, Mom, I need you to listen. Please."

In June of 1968, when I first told her that I was applying to become a CO, her list of worries was so long that I wasn't sure she even heard me. If she did, what I said hadn't registered. She was still shrouded in grief.

With Dad's death, we had stopped functioning as a coherent family. Dad was our sun, and each of us had revolved around him. After his death, we spun off into our own orbits. When we were together, an awkward silence invariably fell as we retreated into mourning, each of us in our own way.

The middle child, Adrienne, had grieved silently. Dad was her idol, and he died just as she approached adolescence. Our younger sister, Cindy, a beauty who had inherited Dad's fair skin and white-blond hair, careened wildly, far beyond Mom's control. Cursed with what we now know as ADHD — attention deficit hyperactivity disorder — Cindy floundered in school, her mediocre performance a stark contrast to the academic success Adrienne and I delivered. After Dad's death, Cindy gained weight, soon suffering ridicule and isolation, her schoolwork dropping even further. She missed Dad in ways I never would be able to understand.

And Mom — Mom was overwhelmed, by the past and the present. She was only in her early forties, still attractive, with a sizzling intelligence that did little to solve her problems. The burdens of financial responsibilities and single parenthood inundated her. Without her Joe, she felt utterly alone in the world.

As for me, in truth, I didn't know what "home" meant anymore. Desperate to find equilibrium, Mom had insisted that we move three times since Dad's death four years ago. The first move was to raise the cash she needed to pay the mountain of medical bills incurred as Dad was dying. Mom was forced to sell our home as fast as she could. She then rented a house nearby, so I could graduate from Clairemont High School.

But remaining in San Diego bruised her emotionally on a daily basis. As soon as she could — after my graduation, in June of 1967 — Mom fled her painful memories of our old life with Dad. Uprooting my sisters and me, she moved us back to her hometown of Seattle, hoping for a new start.

There, however, all of Mom's friends had long-standing marriages, and she couldn't settle into a social circle. When she did meet a man, heartbreak quickly followed. Her father, Grandpa Ben, hired a private detective to look into the background of Mom's suitor. She was devastated to learn that the guy was a grifter who had sensed she was an easy mark.

After that incident we returned to San Diego, where Mom found a home in a Jewish neighborhood. For her, it was an ignominious return into reduced circumstances.

"What is it now?" Quickly reading my agitation, Mom opens with a bitter, raspy assault. "Is this about that goddamned *shiksa*? Is she pregnant?"

I lower my head, placing two fingers of my right hand on my forehead to massage my temples. Mom never misses a chance to denigrate my girlfriend.

"Your fingers are a mess," she snaps. "When are you going to stop biting your nails? You've done that since you were a kid. Why? What could be so bad that you're doing this to yourself?"

In less than a minute, the conversation I had carefully crafted and rehearsed has careened in a different direction. I drop my hands into my lap so Mom can't see how I'm knitting my fingers together so tightly, my knuckles are turning white.

Breaking the tension, she jumps up from the table and resumes a vigorous blitz on the kitchen counter. My shoulders slump and I clench my teeth. For the past year, Mom had become more and more compulsive about cleanliness, going so far as to rip off a piece of waxed paper and place it under a juice glass, lest a sticky circle deface her perfect surface. I worry about her frantic obsessiveness; besides, her neurotic cleaning makes me even more of a stranger in my own home. I've already lost my dad, and now I fear these compulsions are robbing me of my mom.

"Please come back." Now I'm pleading with her. "Sit down, Mom. Enough already with this cleaning. I just need you to listen to me."

She takes her seat again, and I try to regain footing in the conversation. "It's not about my girlfriend, Mom. It's about something else." In her burning gaze, I feel her ceaseless fury that I'm still dating a non-Jewish woman. Any time the topic of my girlfriend of two years surfaces, she finds a way to start a fight. Tension stiffens every muscle in my body as I brace myself.

"Everything you do is about you!" she pounces. "Why don't you ever think about me?"

"Mom, what can I do that I'm not doing?" I throw up my hands in frustration, already prepared to give up.

Whenever I'm around my mother, I sense that she wants me to replace Dad: to meet her needs, to be "the man of the house." But I'm not Dad; I can't fill his role. And when she pressures me, I become enraged, recoiling at her aggression, instinctively withdrawing from her unreasonable demands.

Suddenly, I yearn for the frigid Princeton campus and all the independence and freedom it represents. I've only been here one day, but now I'm wondering if I can go back early. Maybe catch a standby flight right after Christmas, when there will be fewer travelers. Nobody will be on campus — which, at this moment, sounds ideal.

Why do I even *have* to tell her, anyway? I don't need a note from my mother to pursue CO status. After all, I'm a grown man — 20 years old. Not yet a legal adult, but *grown up*.

But then I think it would be so much easier to know I'm not going against her wishes. I hope — I need — to feel that she's behind me, that I have her support... and, indirectly, Dad's.

And so I try again. "Mom — I don't know what to do." I sigh with exasperation, and then I collapse into familiar words that always run through my head. "I miss Dad."

She stops what she's doing, sits down in her chair again, and, dejected, covers her face with her hands. "I know." Her words are muffled, but I hear her. It's a relief that we agree on something. "It's so hard without Dad. I miss him, too. All the time."

"Yes, me too," I say, feeling the weight of the shared loss we rarely discuss. "Especially now."

"Now?" Her head snaps up as she begins to panic. "Why now? What's wrong? Are your grades ok? Are you sick with something, God forbid?" Ever since Dad got sick and died suddenly, at the early age of 42, illness has become the bogeyman who swindled Mom out of her marriage and family.

"Mom, my grades are fine. *I'm* fine." I try to counter her anxieties with a soothing tone. "Please, just listen. Please."

I can see her suffering, how bereft she still is without Dad, and how lonely she is in San Diego. And she's probably right; I *haven't* really thought much about her life.

After all, Mom wasn't always Mom. Before Joe and the kids, she was Zyndell Berliner: young, beautiful, exceptionally intelligent, the only child of immigrant parents.

Her father was a self-made man, a living representation of the American dream. Ben Berliner had no formal education, but he was street-smart. Fleeing Poland, he arrived in Seattle with little more than burning ambition. He started as an itinerant ragpicker and junk-hauler, industriously building his business into the thriving Pacific

47

Iron & Metal. Gifted with foresight, Ben anticipated today's big-box stores and converted an entire floor of his warehouse into a vast discount outlet for second-hand clothing. It became so popular that, on weekends, the police had to direct traffic on the streets surrounding the building.

Grandpa Ben was proud to be prosperous, but he was emotionally impoverished, relying on money as his currency of love.

Zyndell's mother, Grandma Rose, was the second daughter in a family of six children. The family fled pogroms in Russia to land in America, the land of opportunity — but Rose's father quickly stunted his daughter's chances of worldly success. Believing that too much education ruined a girl's prospects for marriage, he pulled her out of school at the age of 12. Rose took a job in one of Seattle's garment sweatshops, where she earned the nickname "Honest Abe" because she never pilfered anything, not even a spool of thread.

Though Ben and Rose shared similar backgrounds, their home — and Zyndell's — was not a happy one. Ben was a philanderer, inflicting hurt that Rose endured for years before demanding a *get,* a formal Jewish divorce. While she might have taken some comfort in the restoration of honesty to her life, this did little to reduce the *shanda* — guilt and shame — she felt at the failure of her marriage in the days when a divorced woman was, quite simply, a scandal.

Her own education thwarted, Rose did everything she could to encourage her daughter's academic achievements. Zyndell thrived in public schools, skipping a couple of grades and graduating from high school at the age of 16. Yet she yearned to be a real American; embarrassed by her mother's heavy accent, Zyndell rarely invited friends to their small apartment, preferring to spend as much time as possible among her friends.

Attending the University of Washington, Mom graduated Phi Beta Kappa before she turned 20. Like all female students, she was steered toward a gender-appropriate major — in her case, home economics.

But, after meeting the handsome, charismatic Joe Wasser at a USO dance, Mom never had a chance to test herself in the world. Married straight out of school, she transferred her strong competitive drive to homemaking and motherhood.

Mom was the brightest of her group of sorority sisters at the U of W. Naturally, all her friends assumed her children would be spectacular. As the first baby in the group, however, I proved to be an embarrassment to Mom. Slow to crawl, walk and talk, I sensed her chronic disappointment in me over the years. Every day, my ineptitudes were a rebuke of her dwindling dreams.

Now, not surprisingly, every conversation I have with Mom is weighted with my lifelong sense of never having lived up to her expectations. This one, too, is certain to lead directly to those familiar feelings of failure.

"Mom, I need to talk with you about the war, about what I've decided to do." I soften my voice, so I won't appear combative or disrespectful.

I press my sweaty hands on the table, fingers splayed. "You know about the lottery, right, Mom?" She nods. "I have a terrible number.... 90."

"90!" Her eyes narrow with fear. "What does that mean?"

"It means after I graduate, I'll be drafted. But I refuse to serve in the military, Mom. I've applied for conscientious objector status. That means I won't fight, but I'll have to serve in some other way."

Relieved that I won't be in combat, she triumphantly concludes, "So, what's to worry? You serve and then go on to law school." For her, our conversation is over. She's about to get up from the table when I motion with both hands for her to stay put.

"Mom, it's not so easy. To become a CO, you have to prove you can't fight due to your religious beliefs. No draft board will grant CO status for men who say they can't fight because of their moral beliefs."

"What then?" Panic jumps back into her voice.

"I can't fight in this war, so I'll refuse induction, Mom. I'll be charged as a felon, as someone who is evading the draft." I now drop the bomb that I know might explode: "I could go to jail."

"Jail!" Anger overtakes fear in her voice. "I'm no fan of this war either, but no son of mine is going to jail to avoid doing what every American man *must* do."

"Mom, you have to understand, this isn't Dad's war." I want her to think about the ambiguities of Vietnam. "In World War II, men were fighting for humanity, but things aren't so clear-cut in this war. I'm not even sure why we're in this mess."

"Not honoring our country?" Now she's bristling, taking my words personally. "I never got in your way when you ran off to the East Coast for college. I'll keep my mouth shut about the shiksa. But this — no! No!"

"Mom, listen to me. I've lost Dad. I *need* you to support me." I'm pleading, but she seems unmoved, utterly unaffected.

I'll have to play the most powerful card I hold. "Mom! I'm your *son!*"

"No! Going up against our country is a disgrace. Your father — by the way, *he* served honorably! Your father would be horrified! Ashamed of you!"

Now she's gathering steam. "It's bad enough to not go in the Army. But jail! Jail is a place for criminals — people who rob! And rape, and... and murder! To do what you're thinking — it's a disgrace — to me, to him, to America. I won't permit it. And if Dad were here, he wouldn't either!"

We sit in silence for a moment, directly across from each other, but never looking at one another.

Then, I dig deep and take the first step toward finding the resolve I'll need. "It's *not* your decision, Mom," I say, steadily and firmly, choking down anger and sadness. "It's mine."

She stands up, noisily shoves her chair back under the table, and returns to the sink to wash her hands, as if she could scrub away the *shanda* of having me for a son. I stand up, carefully pushing in my chair so she won't have to correct another mistake of mine. Leaving Mom's kitchen, I trudge slowly down the hall to my unfamiliar room — now without a father or a mother.

* * *

With little more than a week before I'm due back at Princeton for semester finals, I find myself ruminating endlessly over what to do about my terrible number. Desperate to take some action — anything will do — I consult the listings of government agencies in the green section of the telephone directory, looking for the Selective Service System's phone number.

It's right there. A plain, ordinary phone number. For me, it's an avenue to someone: an actual person who might have some influence over *my* future. Then I notice the address: just up the block from Dad's old office in the Government Services Administration (GSA) building.

My fingers tremble as I dial the number on our harvest-gold wall phone in the kitchen. I have no idea what I'm going to say.

"Selective Service, Draft Board 141. Mary Ann Blaum speaking." This gruff, officious female voice seems to challenge me instantly. Fiddling with the long, squiggly phone cord, heart pounding in my chest, I'm completely tongue-tied, battling the impulse to hang up.

In an instant panic over whether to call this woman "Miss" or "Mrs.," I say nothing. The line buzzes faintly over an awkward silence.

"Hellooo?" She clears her throat. "Are you there?"

"Oh, hello!" I rush in, fearing she'll hang up. "Yes, I'm here."

"Can I help you?"

"Um... yes, mm... Mrs. Blaum." I elect to go with "Mrs.," figuring that won't insult her. "I'm Bruce Wasser. I applied for CO status last year, and, well... I was hoping to come in and talk about my situation."

"Give me a minute to find your file. Please hang on." There's a clattering noise on her end as she puts down the receiver.

And I wait.

After some moments, I wonder if she's ever going to come back. I jump when I hear her voice again: "Mr. Wasser. I see that you are currently attending Princeton University as a full-time student. Is that correct?"

"Yes, ma'am. But I'm calling about my conscientious objector status."

"I'll get to that," she says brusquely. "First, I need to make sure we have all your correct information. We haven't heard from you! Not since June of 1968."

Adrenaline surges through me, and I break out in a cold sweat. Is she telling me I'm doomed because I haven't kept in touch with the draft board? Does my lack of communication make her think I'm not serious — a phony, a fake CO? The board members will probably think I got in touch only after my lottery number was picked.

After I've provided her with every bit of updated pertinent information, Mary Ann Blaum softens just a bit. "Now, what do you need to know, Mr. Wasser?"

I can hear Dad saying, "Don't be fooled by the layout of an office, son. Secretaries run the world." His wisdom suddenly gives me courage.

"Can I come downtown and introduce myself?" I ask boldly. "I have lots of questions, and it would be better if I met you in person."

"Oh!" She's obviously surprised, maybe even flattered. "Not many applicants want to see me, Mr. Wasser. But I'd be happy to meet you. How about next Monday morning, the 29th, at 10?"

"That sounds fine." At least for a moment, I feel quite official. "Is there anything I need to bring with me, Mrs. Blaum?"

"Nothing, as far as I know. Your student deferment will be good as long as you remain a full-time student in good standing. You might want to ask your university to send us your most recent transcript, so we know you're telling the truth. Thank you for calling, and I'll see you on the 29th."

I gently set the receiver on the hook of the wall phone. Now I have a whole new set of worries. How could I have been so stupid as to not keep the board up to date? What else should I have done these past 18 months? What if they reject my application for not doing something I didn't even know I was supposed to do?

* * *

The Saturday before my meeting with Mary Ann Blaum, I find a barber to attack my mop of wavy, collar-length hair. "Get the hair out of your eyes, boy," I hear Dad say in my head. Shorn, I return home and dig through my closet for my navy blazer, my long-sleeved white shirt — dry-cleaned and pristine — and one of the two ties I own. I last wore these clothes three years ago, for my interview with a Princeton Alumni Schools representative. I don't want to appear at the Selective Service office looking, as Dad would say, "Like a *schlub*." Even worse, I don't want to give the impression that I'm part of the growing counterculture that disdains "straight" clothing.

53

On the 29th, I borrow Mom's red Ford Fairlane and drive to the United States Federal Courthouse. I haven't been in downtown San Diego in four years, since my final visit to Dad's nearby office. Much as I want to drop in and say hello to his old coworkers, I know I can't; I wouldn't be able to hold back my tears.

Slowly, as I drive toward the GSA building, I feel Dad's presence and think about all the times he strolled down these sidewalks. "Help me through this, Dad," I say out loud, like a prayer. I stare hard at his old building as I drive past and continue on to the Selective Service office.

A large, framed photograph of President Richard Nixon greets me as I push through the opaque glass door to enter the draft board's office. Beneath the photo sits a woman who must be Mary Ann Blaum, looking every bit as businesslike and serious as the man I detest in the portrait hanging over her head.

The office is distinctly uninviting, gray and bureaucratic, with large metal filing cabinets looming on both sides of her neatly organized desk, and an even larger United States flag standing just behind her chair. Though it's only a few days after Christmas, there's not the slightest suggestion here of the holiday season. No glittering garland, no cheerful Santas, not a single bauble.

As I walk in, she's cradling the phone in her left hand and speaking softly into the receiver. Immediately, I notice she's wearing a wedding band. I celebrate privately that I called her "Mrs. Blaum" when we talked.

After she hangs up the phone, she eyes me up and down appraisingly, and then greets me with a surprising smile. "Hello, Mr. Wasser," she says kindly. "You know, we don't get many young men who visit us here. Most of you consider us 'the enemy.'"

I glance up at Tricky Nixon's beady eyes in his official government portrait.

Then I look back at Mrs. Blaum and, letting loose with all my fears, I talk a blue streak: "Mrs. Blaum, when I made my application two years ago, I didn't really know much about conscientious objection. What I knew was that after Bobby Kennedy and Martin Luther King were assassinated, I could never fight in any war. Violence revolts me, and war is, if nothing else, organized violence. I..."

"Whoa! Hold your horses, Mr. Wasser." She stops me cold and, for the first time in days, I break into a small smile. She sounds like Ben Cartwright on *Bonanza*.

"This isn't the time or place for this." She silences me with a firm tone. "First off, call me Mary Ann. Second, I'm going to tell you what you need to do. Then, I'm going to level with you about your application. Okay?"

"Okay. Sorry, Mrs. — I mean, Mary Ann. I didn't mean to... I mean... I'm worried, and, well, I really don't know what to do—"

She puts up a fleshy palm, like a stop sign. That's when I actually look at her and see her: a calm, earnest, middle-aged woman, slightly overweight, professionally dressed, with simply styled brown hair framing her oval face. She wears a little make-up — not too much — and sports round, wire-rimmed eyeglasses, in the universal John Lennon style.

Are those glasses a hint? A statement? A sign that she may not be as conservative as I fear?

"First," she says, slowly and methodically, "you need to keep us apprised of any changes in your life. Address, phone number, employer, health. Whenever you send a letter to us, make sure you write your Selective Service number on it. Keep a carbon copy for your own records."

Already grateful for her guidance, I nod vigorously. "Yes, thanks. Yes, I'll do that, Mary Ann." I'm still kicking myself for not having contacted the Selective Service over the past 18 months.

"Now, listen carefully, Mr. Wasser, and don't interrupt me."

I stop nodding and give her my full attention, focusing intently on her wire-rims, so I don't miss a thing. I've got to see, hear, and remember everything she says.

"As secretary to the draft board... " Her tone turns official. "I've gotten to know these men who serve on the board very well. They are deeply patriotic, and several have battle scars proving their love of this nation.

"Like me, they believe a strong military is essential for our country. They believe all men should shoulder their responsibilities without complaint or reservation."

Is she telling me that the door is already closed on this option? Is she reprimanding me for even applying? If I can't be a CO, what am I going to do?

"We don't get many applications for CO here," she continues. "Not many Jehovah's Witnesses or Mennonites live in this area. Or maybe it's because San Diego is a military town, and it has a reputation for being tough on CO applicants. Whatever the reason, we just don't get men like you."

She pauses, rifles through the papers on her desk, and says, "I see that you are making a *non-religious* application. Members of our draft board, to a man, are *very* religious. Do you understand what I'm saying here?"

Her loaded phrase, "To a man," slices me into pieces. I swallow hard, my stomach dropping, dread flooding through me. "It would be a good idea for you to write frequently to us about your beliefs. Maybe get letters on your behalf that attest to your character.

"But ..." Now, she peers at me over her granny glasses. "I have to tell you, we have *never* granted a non-religious application for conscientious objection, and I doubt that's going to change.

"If I were you," she says with absolute conviction, "I wouldn't get my hopes up."

January 1970
Reading Period and finals week

"You're on to yourself, Jerome!"

On our first day back at school after winter break, Ric is the first to spot my drastically altered appearance. Clearly amused, he mimes combing his own crew cut with exaggerated swoops, never taking his eyes off my freshly shorn look.

Whenever Ric announces, "You're on to yourself!" I always laugh. At first, it took me a while to figure out what he meant, but now I get it: he's saying that I've found myself, and I'm looking good.

"Nice!" He eyes my cropped haircut, taking me in from every angle. Ric has always worn his brown hair short, a style holdover from his time on the Princeton varsity basketball team.

"But wait!" His eyebrows shoot upward. "Don't tell me you've joined the *establishment*. Let me guess... You're interviewing at IBM? Angling for a junior executive position?"

"No way, Sheldon!"

"Listen, Jerome," Ric whispers conspiratorially as he lifts a tray to carry his breakfast. "Don't worry. I won't tell anyone! It'll be our secret that *you're* joining the Young Americans for Freedom!" That's the squeaky-clean, right-wing campus organization that attracts stuffy conservatives and other Nixon-loving losers.

Ric doesn't talk much about his politics, but every so often, he needles me about my liberal views.

"Yeah, Sheldon, that's it," I nod while grabbing a bowl, a small box of Cheerios, and a carton of milk. "I want to become president so I can show the draft board that I'm not some flag-burning leftie freak."

"Look, Jerome, I get it!" We pull out our chairs at a table by the window, where we might enjoy the view. It's snowing lightly, and I'm a little surprised to realize that the picturesque wintry landscape is more calming than the warm ocean views back in San Diego. It's good to be back at Princeton — and out from under my mother.

"Get what?" I ask, sipping my hot chocolate.

Ric narrows his eyes at me. "Don't take this the wrong way, Bruce, but... One way or another, we all sell out. Sooner or later. It's just a matter of time."

Can he be right? This stops me cold. *Do we all sell out eventually?* I remember when Ric left Princeton's basketball program because he felt the coach wasn't treating every player fairly. He was acting on principle — but now he's talking about abandoning ideals. What about being a lawyer? Will I be selling out if I have a JD next to my name, even if I dedicate my career to helping poor people?

Ric pauses, then changes his tone again. "Ah... I know what's really going on," he grins. "Your mom put you up to this." He gently brushes the bristly top of his head to let me know he's talking about my haircut.

I wince when he mentions Mom. His eyes, shining mischievously when he teased me, suddenly soften. "How'd things go with her during break?"

"Not great, Ric." I look down at my empty cereal bowl. "My mom could barely stand to listen to me. I don't think she has any idea of what's going on. No matter what I said, she either argued with me or ripped me to shreds. And she's *not* going to support me."

Seeing my embarrassment and humiliation, Ric deftly looks away, sparing me further discomfort. "Hey, Jerome." His tone sounds caring. "You've got lots of people here who will line up with you. For what it's worth, I'm one of them."

That *is* worth something: enough to raise my head and look him in the eye. "Ric, what I need right now is a lot of shifts in the kitchen. Can you help me with that?"

"Get that skinny ass of yours down there at lunch today, Jerome. Then basketball at 3 in Dillon?" That's our routine: Every day that we can make it, we play pick-up games in the old gym on campus.

Relieved and grateful, I nod as we stand to get on with the day.

At Princeton, classes end just before winter break, but final exams don't follow immediately. Instead, the university requires students to return for a ten-day Reading Period, during which some professors post new assignments while students cram frantically for final exams.

After Reading Period, finals stretch out over eight days, and there's no juggling of schedules. Each exam is taken, by everyone, at the appointed place and time.

Given how hard I've worked from September to December, this semester's Reading Period offers little value for me, and I know I'll be bored. Worse, all my exams are scheduled toward the end of the exam period, making for a long, long month of waiting.

After breakfast, Ric and I make our way to Firestone, the library that Princeton claims has one of the largest open-stack inventories in all the world. I've spent countless days in this building over the last couple of years, researching the romantic poets, Shakespeare, and Garvey's infamous "Con Interp" legal briefs. But this time, I look hard at the beautiful, imposing stone edifice, and feel dwarfed by its size. I try to comprehend all the information contained in FIrestone's 70 miles of shelves — and, suddenly, I wonder if the library might serve me in another way. Maybe it can provide answers to my gnawing questions. But I have no idea where to start, whom to ask, what to look for.

* * *

On Tuesday, on my way to meet Jim for a walk around campus, I'm struck again by Princeton's winter beauty. Well-tended, shoveled walkways make it easy to get around; crystalline blue skies and bracing cold remind me of how lucky I am to be alive, to be here, with good friends and beloved professors.

"Jim!" I call out when I see him. We fall into an easy pace, walking toward upper campus. Jim is quick to tell me what's on his mind. I'm not surprised that it mirrors what I've been thinking.

"You don't have to say anything, Bruce. This war is destroying everything — our moral reputation, our national purpose, our men. That doesn't even scratch the surface of how it's ripping us apart... our politics, our friendships, our families."

"Jim, I can tell you this, and I can't really tell anyone else." I swallow and plow ahead. "I know, in my heart, I'm a CO But I just don't know how to prove that I can't fight in a war.

"I went to my local draft board." I yank off my orange-and-black skullcap, pointing to my clipped hair. I haven't gotten used to it yet, and my head is actually cold without my insulating mop of curls. "The secretary told me not to get my hopes up."

Trying not to appear shocked at my new look, Jim responds casually. "And... What else did she say? Tell me every detail you can remember."

I summarize my conversation with Mary Ann Blaum. Jim nods, and I notice that as I give him more details, a slight smile tugs at the corners of his mouth. What's *that* about, I wonder.

"Come on, Bruce, don't you see?" Jim looks hopeful. "She opened the door. Not wide — but it's open, nonetheless."

"Uh, that's not how I heard it." I tug my skullcap back over my chilly head. "I mean, she was pretty nice, but San Diego's never had a non-religious CO. And she said that probably won't change. That's exactly what she said."

"I know, but she told you to keep the draft board up to date, which means they're at least *considering* your application. Maybe she's trying to show you how to make those military fanatics on your board take you seriously."

I stop walking and look at him, confused. I'm not following.

"Have you read the *Seeger* decision?" he quietly asks.

I shake my head. What little I know is straightforward: The Supreme Court's 1965 case established that a person can qualify as a conscientious objector without basing his argument on religion.

"That's where you need to start. Read up on *Seeger*."

As Jim turns to walk back to his dorm room, I wonder how he knows so much about conscientious objection... while I know so little.

* * *

The next day, right after breakfast, I head into the bowels of Firestone to look up *Seeger*. Rifling through reference books, I try to figure out what legal volume contains the crucial case. When I finally find *Seeger v. US* 380 US 163 (1965) in the US Reports, I read, then re-read, the decision — unanimous, I notice — of the Supreme Court.

I tell myself to calm down, go slowly, concentrate. Try to figure out how the case applies to me — and to my local draft board.

Three petitioners had claimed that the Selective Service Act had violated their First Amendment rights by insisting conscientious objectors base their claim on "religious training and belief." One petitioner particularly intrigues me — Daniel Seeger.

Seeger objected to war on moral principles and personal ethics, claiming that these beliefs are *similar to* those characterizing a religious faith. He made the case that his "individual training and belief," which included "research in religious and cultural fields," prevented him from fighting in a war. The local draft board found Seeger's beliefs to be "sincere, honest, and made in good faith" — and yet, they denied him CO status. The reason: He didn't avow that his beliefs were rooted in a "Supreme Being," a statutory requirement.

The opinion delved into the history of conscientious objection, of how previous decisions established the need for a conscientious objector to believe in some kind of deity. This court, however, took a different view of the nature of religious belief, expanding the definition of conscientious objection. In doing so, the opinion quoted the highly respected contemporary theologian Paul Tillich, who identified an "ever-broadening understanding of the modern religious community" — one in which belief in God was no longer the sole defining characteristic.

As I re-read the case, one sentence pops off the page. I copy it into my notebook, underlining it three times in red ink. The Court has summarized its new definition of conscientious objection: "The test might be stated in these words: A sincere and meaningful belief which occupies in the life of its possessor a place parallel to that filled by God."

For a long time, I sit motionless. The words, "A place parallel to that filled by God," flash through my mind, over and over. I formulate my

64

own interpretation of these words: A conscientious objector must have a belief so deep, so powerful, that it is *like* a devotion to a deity.

That's me. Though I've stopped going to temple on Friday nights and quietly abandoned most Jewish rituals, I remain proud of my Jewish upbringing and identity. And I'm deeply, genuinely devoted to Jewish ethics.

The core tenet of Reform Judaism — that all of us have an obligation to work toward the messianic vision of a world of peace and justice — has retained every bit of its power in my heart. The prophetic tradition resonates within me; I have tried to live by the idealism of Isaiah, the prophet who foretold the Messiah's coming and brought hope to his people during a bleak and challenging time. I have been inspired by the moral outrage of Amos, a poor shepherd, but a man of thoughtful, fierce integrity.

Above all, each day, I ask myself if I am conforming to the precepts of Hillel, who posed the essential questions: "If I am not for me, who will be for me? And when I am for myself alone, what am I? And if not now, then when?"

Like Daniel Seeger, I have a personal moral code that builds on — and then replaces — a traditional commitment to codified religion. The Jewish principle of *Tikkun Olam* best captures what I want to do with my life: to repair the world, to make whole what is broken.

And now I see that Jim is right: *Seeger* has cracked the door open for my case.

Was Mary Ann Blaum trying to tell me that she understood the implications of the Supreme Court's words? How, then, do I prove my sincerity and beliefs? Who can help me convince the board?

When I finally place the law book back on the shelf, I've completely lost track of time. I check my watch and see that it's 5:45!

"Shit!" I say it out loud. I'm 15 minutes late for my shift at Stevenson. I grab my jacket and briefcase, bolt up the stairs, run out the door and on to Prospect.

* * *

"Hustle, son," I hear my dad's voice ring in my ears as I rush to Stevenson. "Don't ever let 'em see you walkin' when you can run." I shove open the swinging doors to Stevenson's kitchen without taking off my coat and hat.

"Nice you could join us, Jerome!" Ric calls over the noisy gush of running water. He has stepped in for me as the evening's dishwasher. Pointing with a yellow rubber glove at my disheveled hair, he asks, "Were you in the beauty salon?"

"Exactly, Sheldon. I was going for the Ric Singer look. Tried my best, but I was told it just can't be duplicated."

"Cold, man. That's cold."

"Now, if you'll excuse me..." I hang up my coat on the hook by the kitchen door and grab an apron. "I have a shift to complete."

"Actually," Ric raises his eyebrows skeptically. "You had a shift to *start*... at 5:30."

"Move aside, man," I take my spot at the sink, pull on my rubber gloves, and start to tackle the mountain of dirty dishes. "Watch and learn from a pro!"

By 7:30, when my shift grinds to a halt, I'm exhausted and hungry. Cleve, nodding and waving, motions toward me to join him near the stove. As I step toward him, he offers a plate of his famous meatloaf and mashed potatoes, gesturing to me to sit down at his prep table. Then he places a tall, blessedly welcome glass of ice water directly before me, taking a seat across from me.

"Caddy told me what's going on with you, my man," Cleve says softly, looking directly at me. Unsure what he's talking about, I immediately worry that I've disappointed him and Caddy by arriving late to my shift. Just like that, my appetite disappears.

"You know, Caddy really respects you," he says, watching a bead of water run down the side of my glass. I brace myself, fully expecting Cleve to tell me that being late for work is the quickest way to lose Caddy's respect.

Instead, Cleve throws me a curve ball. "So, bro... I know where you stand on this fucked-up war. I hear others talk about you. I know where you're at."

"Cleve... I don't know what's going to happen to me." I shake my head and drop my gaze, just as Cleve looks up at me.

"Look, man, this war is *shit*. The brothers dyin' for nothing. Lies, man, lies... all of it. You know I got family there, guys from where I live. Yeah, we live here, too, y'know? But you students don't know nothin'. Y'all don't care 'bout us and the bros gettin' killed there. The bros shoulder this war. They fightin' way, way more than you white boys."

Blacks, I know, suffer twice as many deaths as whites. Cleve's comment goes straight to Dr. King's "garment of destiny" — the idea that each individual's actions alter the fates of others. I think of Cleve's friends and family — maybe even his sons — and feel queasy with shame and guilt.

"I don't want nothin' to do with this war, just like you." Cleve never takes his fiery, dark eyes off of me. "What the hell we doin' over there? What's the point? And they countin' body bags — like they keep score, who's winning the war! Those bags, man, don't they know? That's somebody's son or dad or brother! That's sick, man. *Sick!* You know what Muhammed Ali said about the war?"

I shake my head in ignorance. All I knew about the world champion boxer, born Cassius Clay, was that he had been stripped of his title because of his opposition to the war. "What's that, Cleve?"

"He said, 'I ain't got no quarrel with the Viet Cong.'" Cleve's eyes burn with rage. "'No Viet Cong ever called me nigger.'"

And then, in a flash, his entire manner changes. He looks across the table, directly at me, and points down to my plate of untouched food. "Now," he says gently, "eat your dinner. 'Fore it gets cold."

* * *

"How did things go over winter vacation, Bruce?" Paul Wagner, a librarian in Firestone's Rare Books Division, looks up to welcome me as I enter the beautiful, highly restricted reading room the next day.

In my "free time," I work ten hours each week as a student assistant in this library-within-a-library, which holds more than 300,000 rare and historically significant books, some dating as far back as the 15th century. My job is to catalog the Stanley Lieberman Memorial Collection of American Juvenile Literature, a hodgepodge of books and magazines from the first decades of the 20th century.

Here, any voice louder than a hushed whisper sounds like raucous cheers during a football game at Palmer Stadium. I'm startled to hear Paul's question — especially since *he* strictly maintains the library's decorum. And then, further suspending his own inflexible rule on talking in the library, he adds a teasing jab: "Make friends with any of the 'America: Love It or Leave It' crowd?"

Paul is a quiet, middle-aged man with a dapper style of dress and a wicked sense of humor. He's referring to a popular bumper sticker that targets Vietnam war protesters, who are perceived as rejecting America itself. Enjoying his own droll remark, Paul's eyes crinkle behind his round tortoiseshell glasses. He looks like an amused owl.

"Absolutely right, Paul. In fact, I'm going to join the 'silent majority' as soon as I can. Any suggestions about a lifetime membership?"

Paul detests Richard Nixon with a contempt matched by few others on campus. As a librarian who has devoted his adult life to the preservation of books and the celebration of intellectual endeavors, Paul especially loathes Tricky Dick's vile, anti-intellectual Vice President, Spiro Agnew, and his penchant for vilifying smart people in general and the media in particular, notoriously branding reporters "nattering nabobs of negativity."

"Things didn't go well over break, Paul," I say. A kind mentor for the past two years, he makes me feel comfortable sharing the latest with him. "And I can't seem to find much information about CO's. The only thing here in Firestone was the legal case."

"You need to get out of Dodge, Bruce. It's a big world out there. Have you thought about going to the New York Public Library?"

Paul doesn't know that I rarely leave Princeton; I simply don't have the money. During my freshman year, I did travel to Philadelphia, where I saw the Celtics play in a rare NBA doubleheader; the following spring, I fulfilled a lifelong dream and saw the Yanks play in the old Yankee Stadium. But going to the Big Apple routinely, drinking in bars that turn a blind eye to fake IDs — that's for the guys who can afford a night out on the town.

But I quickly realize that Paul is right: I need all the information I can get, no matter what the cost. So I grant myself permission and, a few days later, board a 10 a.m. train to Penn Station. In little more than an hour, I'm in New York City.

Trying not to look like the rube I am, I take the barest moment to orient myself, with Madison Square Garden on my left. Then I briskly turn down West 34th Street, passing the imposing Empire State Building. Reminding myself not to gawk, I turn up 5th Avenue — and there it is, the New York Public Library.

The building is enormous: its Beaux-Arts architecture signals stability, purpose and a towering dignity. Much later, I learn that the two imposing marble lions guarding the entryway are named Patience and Fortitude. Two qualities I'll need in the coming months.

* * *

At the circulation desk, the librarian who helps me is something of an old hand. "You're not the first to ask these questions," she says after I explain the purpose of my visit. "Several young men have wondered about becoming a CO Let me take you to the stacks and show you what we have."

In the library's books, I learn that the American public had little sympathy for conscientious objectors during World Wars I and II. The men of conscience who preceded me were labeled unpatriotic, shirkers, slackers, traitors, cowards; their "manhood" was called into question; they were sissies, pansies, faggots. For following their principles, for refusing to fight, these men had been relentlessly degraded, humiliated, and punished.

In the spring of 1917, just before the United States entered World War I, public sentiment ran high against the war. Once the United States began to fight, however, public opinion shifted dramatically, and Americans suddenly disdained COs. Even Eugene V. Debs, the widely respected Socialist presidential candidate, was sentenced to a ten-year prison term for denouncing the war.

During that war, some 65,000 men claimed CO status, most on grounds of religious conviction. Of these, 4,000 were "absolutists" who, like me, refused any participation in war. Many of these men ended up in military prisons where guards tormented them barbarically. Some were forced to stand on tip-toes for eight hours straight; some were shackled by their wrists to the bars of their prison cells. Guards routinely beat COs, stabbed them with bayonets, even dunked them in latrines. Sadistic guards in a Kansas prison subjected objectors to waterboarding. In one military prison, when COs protested the abuse by staging a hunger strike, soldiers retaliated by shoving rubber tubes down their throats to force-feed them.

Just before World War II, Americans were reluctant to get involved, but public opinion reversed overnight when the Japanese bombed Pearl Harbor in December of 1941. Suddenly, with rare unity, the nation supported the war effort — yet, nonetheless, more than 40,000 men registered as conscientious objectors. Many joined the Civilian Public Service or served in the military in non-combatant roles.

Some 6,000 went to jail, comprising an astonishing one-sixth of the entire United States prison population at the time. To prove their patriotism, nearly 500 conscientious objectors volunteered to be "human guinea pigs" for dangerous medical experiments seeking cures for malaria, hepatitis, and typhus. One study, at the University of Minnesota, examined the effects of starvation. These effects, they learned, included lifelong physical and psychological consequences for the participants.

At the end of my day, I shuffle back to Penn Station, shoulders slumped and eyes downcast, my shoes scuffing as I struggle against the sharp wind. On my way to the library, the wind buoyed me toward my mission; now, it's a knife slashing through my jacket. My tightly clenched fist grips my briefcase, stuffed with the bitter fruit of my research.

With all this in mind, I sit silent, barely noticing the wintry landscape in my window as the Northeast Corridor speeds through the New Jersey countryside. Soon I'll be back in Princeton, where I know I can count on plenty of support from my eclectic group of friends. There's Mark Dare, a bitingly funny history major from Carbondale, Illinois, a college town surrounded by cornfields. Dave Brown, from Pompey's Pillar, Montana (population 60), is a driven, idealistic progressive who helped shape Robert Kennedy's presidential campaign in the Rocky Mountain area; and there's Maggie Schwarz, a serious, sensitive pre-med student from nearby New Shrewsbury, New Jersey. At the center of my friendship universe are Ric and Jim.

Among my elders, I rely on Gerald Garvey, whose children anchor me to family life. I've also developed deep friendships with Nancy Joan Weiss, one of the university's first professors in the new Department of Afro-American Studies. This is Princeton's first attempt at inclusion, and I'm proud to have helped bring it into existence as part of a student-faculty initiative in the fall of 1969. Eric Goldman, whose work drew me to Princeton and who would become my senior thesis advisor, and his wife, Jo, have repeatedly invited me to spend time at their Princeton townhouse. The Goldmans have no children, which I'm sure is one reason they've been so welcoming to me.

Much as I treasure these friendships with my professors, rising above them all is the bond I've developed with Martin Duberman, a radical leftist historian. Duberman has challenged me to view everything, particularly my own life, through a different lens.

Then, I've come to trust and love Caddy and Cleve. All I need from Caddy is a quick nod — an almost unnoticeable movement — that telegraphs his paternal concern. I feel Cleve's companionship and approval, too, and we identify with each other as outsiders.

Yet, even as I recognize my good fortune in having these friends, I remind myself that Princeton is self-contained, smugly insulated, and far removed from the larger world. This community — even with all its elitism and pressures to conform — will be more tolerant of my resistance than anywhere else.

Americans harbor a deep, often vicious hostility toward men like me. My day in the New York Public Library has shown me, with chilling clarity, how my country has regarded COs through two world wars, and how they're viewed today.

The train's wheels clickety-clack rhythmically along the rails in a drumbeat of doom. I wonder: Do I have the courage to live the rest of my life branded as a cowardly pariah?

As the spring semester of my junior year starts, popular music and its lyrics thrum with the discontent, anger and hope that so many on campus are feeling. Crosby, Stills, Nash & Young's elegiac "Teach Your Children" offers solace to those alienated from their parents, yet still hoping to connect: "Teach your parents well; their children's hell will slowly go by." Creedence Clearwater Revival's "Fortunate Son" vibrates with outrage, declaring "it ain't me" who will wave the flag or fight the war. Even the previously apolitical Rolling Stones call for violent revolution in "Street Fighting Man," mocking the futility of "compromise solution."

Everywhere I look, Princeton's undergraduates are exploring an array of answers to the vexing problems of racism and war. A group of Black students is exploring the creation of a "Community House" project that will connect undergrads with low-income minority children who live in and around the town of Princeton. Angry anti-war students are focusing their ire on the Institute for Defense Analysis (IDA), a research program housed on campus that has come to symbolize America's militarism.

Surrounded by my furiously opinionated, loudly outspoken peers, I feel like the only one who's floundering. I wonder who I am, how I can influence political change, and what I can do to end this damnable war. Am I just gutless, afraid to throw myself into the growing anti-war movement on campus? Am I so short-sighted and self-protective that I ignore the hypocrisy of maintaining my student deferment? Would I be welcomed or shunned by Blacks if I try to help organize the Community House project?

Whatever path my mind follows, I hit the roadblock of fear. Nothing, right now, is more important to me than achieving CO status. I'm convinced that any misjudgment, any misstep or run-in with authority, will destroy my application. I live in constant fear of that failure. Fear of not living up to my own moral code. Fear of disappointing my father.

Still, I need some way to express my outrage about the war, some way to protest — and that's how I find myself at a meeting of Princeton's chapter of the Students for a Democratic Society (SDS) in early February, during the first week of classes. Some of my History Department friends encouraged me to attend, insisting that this new political organization offers hope. SDS, whose network of local chapters is growing rapidly on college campuses across the country, has a reputation for generating ideas to pressure the government to withdraw from Vietnam.

My evening shift at Stevenson ends after the meeting has started, so I have to hustle across campus to one of Princeton's countless wood-paneled classrooms. As I enter the stuffy room, a good fifteen minutes late, pungent smells greet me — stale sweat, cigarette smoke, the musty tang of marijuana — all familiar, but concentrated and reeking in this crowded space. Almost everyone is wearing a counterculture uniform of sorts: fringed suede jackets, leather necklaces dangling peace signs, elaborately beaded headbands. In my well-worn wool coat over a faded Princeton sweatshirt, I look like an establishment figure's poor cousin who lost his way and stumbled into a radical political-action meeting.

Taking a seat in the back of the room, I try to sort out disparate threads of discussion. There's talk of "capitalist pigs," "revolution," "repressive tolerance."

"Marcuse has it right!" one student pundit tells the group. "No free speech for fascist pigs. When that pig Hickel comes here..."

Utterly confused, I nudge the guy sitting next to me and whisper, "Who's Marcuse? What's he talking about?"

I've never seen this guy on campus, have no idea who he is. He glares at me before hissing, "Don't you know anything, man? Marcuse is right on. Free speech isn't free, y'know. Fascist pigs don't have the right to speak here." He nods his head so vehemently that his red paisley bandana loosens, allowing a few curls of frizzy brown hair to pop out. I look at him blankly, and he rolls his eyes, clearly exasperated by my unfathomable ignorance.

Later, I read Herbert Marcuse, who — in the name of freedom — calls for silencing advocates of right-wing positions, arguing that their voices only intensify repression of marginalized groups. I'm repulsed by this Orwellian commentary on free speech; I deeply embrace the First Amendment's protections of expression. I had thought that everyone on the Left shared my view. Not anymore, I guess.

During the meeting, I gather that SDS is planning a protest against the upcoming lecture by Walter Hickel, Nixon's ecology-minded Secretary of the Interior. SDS isn't critical of Hickel's protective position on the environment, but the group wants to taunt him about his presumed support for the war. The discussion explores ways to disrupt his speech, looking to agree on the most effective and dramatic tactic.

The next item on the meeting's agenda — taken up without a clear plan for the Hickel speech — is the question of which revolutionary figure best serves as inspiration and role model for the upcoming Armageddon. This topic incites the audience.

"Che! Che! Che!" one frenzied voice yells fervently from the back of the room. He's promoting the recently murdered Latin American icon, Che Guevera, a physician who became a major figure of the

Cuban Revolution and is increasingly a counter-culture symbol of rebellion.

"Fanon!" Another voice shouts out another name I don't recognize. "Read Fanon if you want a clue about what to do." Later, I learn that Frantz Fanon was a Black psychiatrist from the French colony of Martinique. His influential books, *Black Skin, White Masks* and *The Wretched of the Earth*, decried the destructive impact of colonialism on Third World peoples. Violence, he believed, was the only language colonists truly understand, and the only way for the colonized to regain a sense of self, culture, and statehood. Like Che, Fanon died young — although of pneumonia, not execution.

"No way," another yells, "Ho [Chi Minh] is the man." Gathering steam, this SDSer shouts louder. "Ho transformed North Vietnam. He ain't afraid to get rid of reactionary elements."

There's no dialogue here; nobody is listening to anybody in this inchoate one-upping contest. Ironically, the raucous room reflects Princeton's hyper-competitive culture, a constant state in which students jockey relentlessly to be acknowledged as the best — in this case, the most radical.

Unnoticed in the commotion, I make my way to the door, now convinced that when the revolution comes, Jim and Ric and I will all be lined up and shot for our "counter-revolutionary beliefs."

In the cold night air, walking slowly back to my dorm room in Patton Hall, I realize I'm completely disenchanted with the New Left, which demands a radical transformation of American society, repudiating the legacy of President Kennedy and his New Frontier in favor of some kind of Marxist revolution. As I understand it, the "Old Left" brought into being once-radical proposals that are now pillars of the liberal establishment, spanning several decades between the social programs of Franklin Roosevelt's New Deal in the 1930s to the sweeping reforms of Lyndon Johnson's Great Society, enacted just a few years ago. The New Left claims that today's liberal America is a failure, its efforts against racism feeble and inadequate, its moral compass fatally compromised by militarism, big business, political repression and cultural sterility.

I think about how these extremists have no love for the United States and its foundational democratic principles. Rather, they rejoice in demonstrating to one another how much they despise America. Yet I don't see *them* dropping out of school, going to Cuba or China or North Vietnam to hasten the coming of a new age. Just as much as the right wing offends me, with its "America — Love It or Leave It" mentality, these SDSers scare me. Barely in their 20s, they're hardened and rigid in their arguments, as unbending as the ossified members of the establishment they despise.

Sure enough, about a month later, anti-war protesters disrupt the event when Walter Hickel addresses an audience of more than 2,000 in the new Jadwin Gymnasium. Tension is palpable as Hickel delivers his formal talk while Princeton's president sits stonily to his left.

The suspense snaps when some 75 protestors — dressed as Halloween-style "Indians," red paint smeared on their faces — burst into the gym, shouting "war whoops" to upend the question-and-answer session.

To me, this display is appalling. These SDSers seem to believe that imitating the ugliest Western movie stereotypes will hasten an end to the war in Vietnam. They're a bunch of affluent, dumb white kids, insulting and exploiting marginalized people with their juvenile behavior. "Fatheads," I hear Dad's voice in my head.

Still, at least one thing is now clear. Any lingering pull I may have felt toward the New Left has evaporated.

* * *

At Princeton, one particular father figure will have a deep and lasting influence on my life. Martin Duberman, in his early 40s, is a campus icon. Slender, usually dressed in unprofessorial turtleneck sweaters and bell-bottom pants, the man magnetically attracts those on campus yearning for change, in part by taking a generous personal interest in his students' lives. He is an iconoclast whose intellectual dissent underscores the disconnect many students feel in a society warped by violence and prejudice.

In the classroom, he speaks with uncommon eloquence while inviting questions and dialogue, rejecting the formalities of lectures and dogmatic pronouncements. By 1970, Martin has become a symbol of pedagogical rebellion; his course on American radicalism completely abandons the rigid organization of other history courses — no tests, no syllabus, no written papers. He doesn't even take attendance. Encouraging his students to follow their own interests, he rejects the sterility of conventional instruction, instead holding the radical idea that education must unite, not separate, intellect and emotion — the head and the heart.

When I first met Duberman as a student in his course on the Civil War, I was a star-struck sophomore. A revisionist historian, he cast 19th century abolitionists as idealistic advocates for social justice, bucking a century of conventional historians' condescending disdain for these anti-slavery activists. All of us recognized Professor Duberman as a voice against racism and intolerance.

Last year, I'd sat in the front row and hung on his every word. About every five minutes, I would raise my hand to ask a question, calling out, "Professor Duberman, Professor Duberman!" After a few weeks, he took me aside after class and, to my shock, told me to call him Martin. This familiarity eliminated the usual distance and power imbalance in the professor/student relationship, and the change emboldened me to pursue a closer relationship with him.

Now, in the tumultuous spring of 1970, I spend as much time as I can with Martin. It's not easy, as he is one of the few professors who doesn't live near campus, and he has only limited office hours: Tuesday and Thursday, 2 to 4 p.m. I make a practice of sitting outside his second-floor office in Dickinson Hall, seizing any opportunity to spend time with him.

It's no wonder students adore him. When we talk, his wide-set gray-blue eyes seem to burrow into me. His thick, wavy brown hair is combed back from a broad forehead; his face curves onto a gracefully squared jaw. With Martin, I can engage in serious, reflective conversation; the more time I spend with him, the more comfortable I am in his presence.

One April afternoon, I drop my defenses to reveal parts of myself that I've tried to bury during my time at Princeton. "Martin, I... I feel like a failure," I falter. "Everyone else here seems to have their shit together. They know what they want, and they know how to get it. Me... I'm lost. I'm —"

Brow furrowed, he shakes his head and calmly interrupts me. "Bruce, where is all this coming from?"

He waits patiently for my answer. Biting my lip, I wonder, where do I begin? My father's death, my mother's rejection, my sense of family-lessness, homelessness, my alienation at Princeton. Instead of answering him, I hold up my hands to show him the shame I try to hide from everyone else — my badly bitten fingernails. "Look, Martin," I say, "I'm a mess. Look at me, I worry all the time."

"Who made you feel so bad about yourself?" Just like that, he cuts to the core.

I can't bring myself to say the word out loud, so I say nothing. But I know the answer: it's God. I feel my father's death, when I was only 15, is my punishment for something I must have done — some wayward behavior, some profound personal inadequacy.

"I know you're intense, Bruce," Martin continues. "That's one of the things I like about you. But we all have our torments. Why are you so anxious? Why so hard on yourself?"

Why? It's how I've coped. I've driven myself to excellence to compensate for the loss of my father, as if excellence could insulate me from pain and suffering, as if my accomplishments could prove that I never deserved this terrible deprivation. As if — if only I could be good enough — my efforts might resurrect my father and restore my life to its former equilibrium.

But no. Now I see that my drive is a childish attempt to control a cruel, uncontrollable world where anything can happen at any moment. A world where someone could lose his strong, healthy, athletic 42-year-old father to a brief illness. A world where we murder our greatest leaders. A world where a fatherless young man could draw "90," a terrible lottery number, and be forced to forfeit his future, to fight in a war he abhors. My urge to steer the events in my life — especially with the added, overwhelming complication of the war — has exhausted me, taken me to a dark place where I can't find my way out.

Martin's kind eyes reflect deep concern. He sees how his question has agitated me. "Take a few deep breaths," he says quietly. "Don't say anything for a few minutes. "

Until this moment, I've never experienced what's known as focused breathing. I do what Martin says, slowly inhaling and exhaling. He encourages me to continue this pattern for what feels like minutes, maybe hours. I lose myself to my breathing. In time, something shifts in me and, finally, I feel less pressure in my chest.

"Now," he says, when he senses that I'm calmer, "tell me your greatest fear."

"I'm worried I won't become a CO, Martin," I say, listing all the negative thoughts that have run through my head for months. "I'm afraid

I'll end up in jail, and I won't be able to become an attorney. I won't have the chance to defend people I might help."

"Bruce, you're smart enough to know that a lot of good people — people like you, who love this nation — have gone to jail for their beliefs. I was arrested for protesting the war in a sit-in at the US Senate. All of us find a way — not despite, but *because of,* our jailing — to work for our beliefs. You'll need to make peace with that idea."

"There's more." I clench my teeth to keep my emotions in check. "I miss my father." My voice breaks, but I can't stop now; the words spew out of me. "So many guys here say awful things about their dads. They'll say, 'He's such an asshole!' or 'I hate my father!' or 'Fuck him!' When I hear them, I think, 'Fine! Let's trade places. I'll take my dad back, and you can see what it feels like to live without yours.' It's terrible, Martin, but that's what I think."

Despite my efforts, tears roll down my cheeks. Martin comes out from behind his desk, puts his arms around my shoulders, and holds me close. The last man to hug me was Caddie, on the night of the lottery. This embrace, equally unexpected, feels just as loving and monumental.

"I want to do well by my country, Martin." I'm crying softly into his shoulder. "But I also have to live with myself."

"I can't bring your father back, Bruce," he says into my ear. "No one can. I'm sorry. So sorry this happened to you."

After a few minutes, Martin releases me, walks back behind his desk, takes his seat. Then he leans forward and looks intently at me. "But I can give you some advice about change. You can't take this on all by yourself. You can only do your part.

"As my beloved grandmother used to say..." He breaks off his intense gaze, looking into the distance, as if he's counseling both of us. "'One bird alone cannot bring the spring.'"

SPRING BREAK, LATE MARCH 1970

"Mom, I'm not a kid anymore."

It's an effort, but I'm speaking as calmly as I can, squinting at my mother. The last time I saw her was just a few months ago, but she's made a big change in her appearance since winter break.

Again, we're sitting opposite each other at her kitchen table, arguing over my terrible draft number. She's behaving in the same belligerent manner. We've picked up exactly where we left off.

So — what's different?

Mom has a few more creases around her eyes, but more notably, she's changed her hair color. After Dad's death, her once-lustrous brown curls lost their sheen. Now, she's a reddish blonde.

I guess she thinks it's attractive. Maybe all her friends love it. But, to me, it's strange and disorienting. She doesn't look like my mother anymore; she's not the mom I know.

"I need you to listen to me, Mom."

"I need *you* to listen to *me*," she snaps back. "I want you to know, I took things into my own hands. Malcolm didn't think I should do it, but I'm your mother and I did what I think is best."

"You *what?*" I gasp, dreading her answer. "What did you do?"

But before she has a chance to answer, the phone rings. She picks up and starts chatting with a friend about plans for a weekend movie. They're going to see "Airport," a disaster movie. I wonder why, with all the catastrophes in her life, she'd find this entertaining.

As I sit silently, listening to her casually debating matinee versus evening show, my anxiety gnaws and grows. I can't *imagine* what she did. Maybe she talked to our rabbi. Or polled her friends in the synagogue sisterhood about what *they* think I should do. Maybe she asked my doctor to concoct a medical excuse to get me out of military service.

But if Malcolm tried to dissuade her — that makes me worry. Malcolm Lichtenstein is a very nice, practical man whom she's been dating for the past few months. I met him during winter break, and my impression, though brief, was nothing but good. Physically the opposite of Dad, Malcolm is a small-framed, curly haired Brooklyn Jew. He's a bright, good-natured guy, and I think he has brought some joy into Mom's life. Their relationship has grown more serious; I have the feeling he steadies her.

As for my own interests, I suspect he'll give her good advice on whatever she was considering. He's some sort of psychologist, so I'm guessing he would tell her to be cautious about getting mixed up with her kids' affairs.

But he's not a miracle worker — and, sadly, our family, now more splintered than ever, appears to need just that.

My younger sister, Adrienne, now attends Western Washington University, leaving Mom alone with Cindy, her youngest and most challenging child. While Adrienne has the ability and patience to handle Mom, Cindy fuels her symptoms of depression and neurotic compulsivity. Cindy's life is in a downward spiral: still gaining weight, falling apart in school, hanging out with unruly boys Mom can't stand.

At last, Mom hangs up the phone and heads back to the kitchen table. "Mom, you can't live my life," I say as she takes her seat. "I just need you to listen and try to support me."

"That's exactly what I'm doing, Bruce. Supporting you! That's why I spoke with Congressman Wilson's office about your situation."

"You *what?!*" Instantly I jump out of my seat, practically yelling at her. "'Slobbering Bob' Wilson? *Why* did you do *that?*" San Diego's US Representative, Robert Wilson, is a venal, brain-dead Republican whose politics I detest.

"I looked into getting you classified as a 'sole surviving son'." She realizes that she's wildly overstepped here: her voice is actually shaking, and she avoids looking at me. "To get you out of the war."

Stunned as I am, I recall that, in 1964, recognizing that sons of World War II veterans were reaching draft age, Congress changed the Selective Service Act to exempt from military service the only surviving son of a family in which the father died as a result of military service. But Dad died in 1965, of cancer. It's a complete distortion of his illness to claim it resulted from his wartime service at Fort Lewis, Washington.

"Mom! Jesus Christ, Mom! Why? *Why?*" I seethe and sputter. "You know Dad didn't die from war wounds. How could you do this without even *asking* me?"

"Because of this *mashugana* CO business, that's why," she replies — trying to sound firm, but still avoiding my eyes. "That's just not going to work! The Congressman's office doesn't think you have any chance, either. And my friends at the temple all think I'm doing the right thing," she adds, as if my future is up for some kind of vote by the sisterhood.

I'm stunned, almost dizzy, a thumping pressure suddenly erupting in my head. Is she so oblivious that she doesn't realize that her call may have *hurt* my chances of becoming a CO? Will the board now see me as a pathetic baby who needs his mommy to do his work for him? "Shit. Shit. *Shit!*" I mutter to myself.

Working to calm down, I quickly decide that I need to talk to Mary Ann Blaum. She can help me assess the damage. Maybe even convince the draft board that I had nothing to do with Mom's call to the congressman.

Slumping into my chair, I look across at her, and my heart sinks. I see the worry on her face — the fear that she's going to lose me, just as she lost her Joe. It hurts to take in her pain, and I ask myself: What kind of son would cause so much torment to his mother?

But then, just as quickly, I feel the burn of my own rage: Why does she continue to treat me like a 15-year-old boy? How can she hold on so tightly? Why won't she let me grow up?

* * *

Today is Thursday; I return to Princeton Saturday, but I'm desperate to meet with Mary Ann Blaum before I go. When I call her immediately after learning what Mom has done, she agrees to see me in her office on Friday. Once again, I put on my one and only sports coat. In an effort to look fresh, I rummage around and find a different tie. On this visit, however, I don't have time to get a haircut, so I look a little shaggier.

As I enter the Selective Service Administration's office, Richard Nixon's beady eyes stare down at me again. I shudder with fear and embarrassment. I don't have any idea of how I can explain this situation to Mary Ann Blaum. How can I convince her that I had *nothing* to do with my mother's actions?

Mary Ann looks up from her desk and says, "You're looking good today, Bruce. Quite stylish."

"Thanks, Mary Ann." Her compliment derails me; I was about to dive in with some sort of explanation.

"Almost good enough to get a summer job here." She chuckles at her joke. Then, pretending her two fingers are a pair of scissors, she reaches out, acting as if she's cutting my hair.

This makes me laugh, taking the edge off my nerves. "I don't think you'll want me after you hear what I'm about to tell you."

She waves away my comment and remarks tersely, "I already heard!"

"You did?" Now I feel sick. Immediately, I blurt out, "Mary Ann, there's no way I would have asked my mother to contact Congressman Wilson." My words sound rehearsed, lame, unconvincing. "I hope you know that. I would be too embarrassed to come in here today if I'd done that. I mean... I'm embarrassed as it is. Actually, I'm mortified —"

"Slow down, Bruce," she says.

"You know how sincere I am about my application," I press, unable to stop myself. "I would never do anything like that."

"Look, Bruce, I don't think you put your mother up to this." I see a flash of compassion in her eyes. "That's not how I read you."

"Thank you!" I take a deep breath. "I was so worried you wouldn't believe me."

"But really, a sole surviving son?" She raises her eyebrows skeptically. "In your case, I'd say, that's a bit of a stretch."

"I know," I bite my lip and shake my head. "I don't know how my mother came up with that. It's humiliating!"

"I'll tell you," she says, "this isn't the first time a panicked mother or father tried to bend the rules to help their son. I get these calls all the time."

She looks down at a photograph on her desk, probably of her own family and, for a moment, retreats into her thoughts. Maybe there's someone she loves who could be drafted.

Bringing herself back, Mary Ann looks me in the eye again. "I know this war isn't the most popular song on the Top 40."

I smile at her quip.

"But in this office," she turns her hand up, "we are responsible for following the law. The Selective Service looks down on anyone —no matter how much power he or she may have — who tries to influence us.

"In fact, tampering," she hesitates a little, then speaks more emphatically, "trying to *force* us to act in a certain manner actually has the opposite effect. It damages an applicant's chances."

"I understand," I say. "That's why I wanted to come in today. I was hoping —"

Her phone rings and stops me from saying anything else. "Excuse me. Let me get this, Bruce." She picks up the receiver and punches one of the clear buttons lining the base of her black phone. "Selective Service. May I be of assistance?"

I sit still on the other side of her desk, fighting the urge to fidget, to pick at my nails or crack my knuckles. Mary Ann isn't saying much while her caller is going on and on. I can't make out the words, but I wonder if the caller is yet another mother trying to "tamper."

After hanging up the receiver, Mary Ann reveals nothing about the call, picking up right where she left off with me. "I'll be honest with you, Bruce. Your mother having Congressman Wilson contact us doesn't help your case. It's bad on two fronts: it makes you look insincere about your CO application, and you look like you can't handle your own business."

"Mar ... Mary Ann," I stammer, "I know. I mean, I don't know *what* to say. I'm —"

She holds up her hand to stop me and says softly, "I'll do what I can to straighten this out for you."

"Thank you," I say with gratitude. "I really appreciate it."

"But let me say this." Her tone, even her posture, now shifts from sympathetic to stern.

"I'm not oblivious to what's happening outside these doors. All the protests, draft-card burning, marches. We even have picketers in front of our office. Nobody — and I mean *nobody* — is going to pressure us and sway our decisions.

"But you need to be careful out there. Don't get into any run-ins with the law. If you get arrested, it will kill your application."

"Yes, I know." When she stands, so do I. "Thanks, Mary Ann."

This conversation is somewhat reassuring; I'm sure Mary Ann can see that I've relaxed a little. Although I can't erase what Mom did, at least I have someone in the office who's looking out for me and my application. Still, I've got to make sure Mom never interferes again.

I extend my hand to Mary Ann. She takes it, smiles, and says, "And if you're serious about working here next summer, do something about that hair, would you?"

* * *

The next day, I intentionally avoid Mom before catching a standby red-eye to New York. I have to talk to her once more about her call to Congressman Wilson, but I'm dreading it. Instead, I spend the day in my room — packing, calling friends, doing some reading.

In the early evening, when she and I sit down together for a quick dinner, I know this is my moment. Hoping to leave without another bitter argument, I tell myself to stay calm and carefully consider my words. When I look across the table at her, I see fear and worry in her eyes. That's probably what she sees in mine.

"Mom, I know you meant well by calling Congressman Wilson." I'm acknowledging her good intentions before I make my request. "But it backfired. You see that, right?"

"Backfired?" She knits her eyebrows and scowls at me.

"Yeah, Mom. First, you and I both know that I don't fit into the 'sole surviving son' category, since Dad died of cancer. And I talked to the Selective Service people, and they consider your call to Congressman Wilson tampering. It may have hurt my chances of becoming a CO."

"That wasn't tampering." She narrows her eyes, maintaining her rigid stance.

"So I'm asking you — no — I'm *begging* you not to interfere anymore."

"That may be how *you* see it," she snaps, ready to re-engage in battle. "But I'm doing what's best for my son. I want to keep you alive!"

I take a few deep breaths, forcing myself not to take the bait. Ever since Dad's death, Mom worries constantly about losing one of her children. She doesn't see her actions as trampling on reasonable boundaries; she believes she's taking simple, necessary steps to keep me safe.

I stay calm and stick with my message: "For my sake, Mom, I want you to promise me you won't take things into your own hands again."

"I hear what you're saying." To my relief, I hear compassion in her voice. Maybe she, too, is trying to avoid parting with harsh words. But then she quickly adds, "I just can't promise you that!"

I resist the urge to throw up my hands, stifling the impulse to argue. There's simply no reasoning with her. Maybe I just have to accept that she's going to meddle, and all I can do is limit what she knows. From now on, I won't give her any information about my application — either successes or failures.

She rises and beckons with her head: time to get in the car to go to Lindbergh Field. Then she stops, glaring at me, as if I've attacked her.

"You simply can't ask me not to do what I know is best," she insists. "That goes against all of my instincts."

Underscoring her point, she adds, "You *can't* ask me to stop being your *mother!*"

APRIL **1970**

In this wartime spring, Princeton, like other campuses across the country, is a pressure cooker whose release valve is stuck shut. Anger foams, froths, boils over. Students search desperately for ways to express their rage and frustration over the war.

In daily demonstrations, the most radical voices on campus shout revolutionary slogans like "Ho, Ho, Ho Chi Minh, NLF is gonna win." NLF is the National Liberation Front, whose South Vietnamese guerrilla soldiers join North Vietnamese troops in fighting against South Vietnam's forces. *South* Vietnamese soldiers fighting *other* South Vietnamese soldiers only worsens the battlefield confusion in the jungles of that ravaged land. Yet SDS and other anti-war groups readily adopt catchy slogans glorifying conflict, with never a thought about the hideous reality of war.

Our frayed, angry nation seems to be imploding, and I feel like I am, too. Though I'm utterly disgusted with my country's indefensible actions, I'm paralyzed, forbidden to protest — because now, I know for sure that if I commit even one misstep, my CO application will be doomed. All I can do is establish myself as an official "objector." I'm scared all the time. For myself, and for the nation I love.

Except for a few campus conservatives, everyone here detests Nixon. All through 1968, he ran for President on a promise: a "secret plan" to end the war. A polarized nation handed him a narrow victory, more to repudiate Lyndon Johnson than to affirm any Republican ideas.

Once he took office, Nixon's "secret plan" vanished. Far from ending the war, the new President not only continued LBJ's ruinous Vietnam policies in Vietnam, he actually escalated the war. Nixon's approach, appropriately named the "Madman Theory," aimed to intimidate leaders of hostile Soviet-bloc nations by portraying the President as irrational and volatile — a man not to be provoked, for fear of an unpredictable American response.

It sounded like a bizarre fantasy, but on the ground, reality was just as weird. Nixon believed that "more" — more troops, more massive bombing — would force the North Vietnamese to surrender, choosing to negotiate a peace settlement instead of being obliterated.

One year after his inauguration, however, Nixon had nothing to show for his efforts but more body bags.

I'm convinced that things can't get any worse, but I'm wrong. Nixon is now ramping up hostilities by sending 2,000 American combat troops to invade Cambodia, a neutral country that shares a long border with Vietnam. He also orders B-52 bombers to begin direct hits on North Vietnamese bases.

To me, the invasion of Cambodia proves that the Madman Theory is real. Nixon's increasingly aggressive bombing is sickeningly inhuman. Just as bad is the simple fact that it's unlikely to work.

On April 30, Nixon appears on nationwide television to explain his decision to invade Cambodia. Even the Trekkies in Stevenson recognize the importance of this moment; they cede control of the TV to concerned students who want to watch "Tricky Dick" justify his decision.

Unlike the raucous night when lottery numbers were announced, the upstairs television room is gloomy and quiet. We're stunned into silence as Nixon — looking directly at the camera, a serene sincerity replacing his usual scowl — presents his mind-blowing argument: invading Cambodia is not *expanding* the war, but actually *ending* it.

"The areas in which these attacks will be launched are completely occupied and controlled by North Vietnamese forces," he explains. "Our purpose is not to occupy the areas. Once enemy forces are driven out of these sanctuaries, and once their military supplies are destroyed, we will withdraw."

Immediately after hearing Nixon's Orwellian justification for his Cambodian operations, students across the nation spring into action, working to formulate an appropriate response. At Princeton, thousands of students and faculty gather spontaneously, swarming into the University Chapel. The imposing church, more cathedral than chapel, has a capacity of about 2,000 people — but, right now, it looks like it'll be overcrowded.

I stop and watch for several minutes, trying to decide what to do. Part of my hesitation is the fact that I can't stand the chapel. The one time I set foot in it was for a required freshman convocation in the early fall of 1967. It was my introduction to Princeton's deep hypocrisy. I promised myself back then that I'd never again enter its pious sanctuary.

The majestic power of the chapel is indisputable. The massive edifice, completed in 1928, reflects a 14th-century English Gothic architectural style. Of its counterparts worldwide, only the chapel at King's College, Cambridge University, is larger.

The Tiffany stained-glass windows depicting the Blessed Virgin Mary, the infant Jesus, and various saints; the engravings on the pews memorializing the music, scholars and teachers of the Christian church; even the testimonial stones on the walls — every element of the chapel immerses visitors in the university's muscular Christian heritage.

Princeton calls the chapel an ecumenical space, open to all. But its overbearing Christian symbolism, lacking even the smallest gesture toward ecumenism, strikes me as implicitly hostile to anyone who doesn't embrace a Christian religion.

The chapel is famous for its classical beauty, a must-see on any campus tour. In a single building, it distills what Princeton thinks of itself: imposing, proud, perfect.

For me, the chapel is a silent, constant reminder that I'm an outsider — by character, by class, by faith. Its hulking presence announces: "You are a guest here, and not an especially welcome one. You'll never belong here. You may dress like us, talk like us, act like us — but you'll never be one of us."

Now, watching the outraged throngs pushing through those heavy oak doors on their ornate ironwork hinges, I feel the sharp tug of responsibility. I, too, desperately want to make my voice heard against the war.

But then I shrug it off. Instead, I head to my usual destination — *my* temple, located right next door to the chapel — Firestone Library.

I will not be one of them. Not tonight, not ever.

* * *

In the morning, Ric and I meet as usual at Chancellor Green. He takes a quick look at me across the breakfast table and asks, "You going on strike, Jerome?"

"Strike? What the fuck are you talking about, Ric?"

"I can't believe Mr. Anti-War doesn't know what happened last night!" A smile plays at the corners of his mouth. "The chapel was *electric* last night. Where were you, anyway? I called your room and looked for you. Couldn't find you anywhere."

"Firestone. I went there right after my shift. But what happened last night? What's going on?"

"Jerome, the campus voted to strike... an immediate strike!"

"Strike! What the hell does that mean?"

"You *do* know what Nixon said last night, right?" he says sarcastically, narrowing his eyes.

"Ric, I was in the TV room at Stevenson, too. Remember? I saw you across the room; I nodded to you." Then the word "strike" sinks in. I swallow hard, feeling as if there's a noose tightening around my neck. "Does that mean everything's shutting down?"

"Nobody knows." Ric shrugs. "That's why everyone's getting together next week at Jadwin — Monday, I think — to figure it out. But I know this much: it ain't business as usual here anymore, Jerome. That's for sure. I don't think anybody's going to class today."

"Not going to class?" I'm shocked. To my knowledge, Princeton has never shut down, for *any* reason, in its history.

I don't have any classes on Friday, so there's nothing for me to boycott. Then I remember my scheduled shift tonight, at 5 p.m., at Stevenson. Does a strike mean I'm not supposed to work in the kitchen? I can't afford to boycott my job — not only for financial reasons. It would be personal, too — like turning against Cleve and Caddie, my Princeton family.

But I can't just sit on the sidelines, either. I don't know what to do.

Where's Jim? Maybe he can help. Jim has emerged on campus as one of the most principled voices against the war. He's a member of the National Student Strike Committee, a nationwide ad hoc group of students outraged by Nixon and dedicated to doing something on campus to express our hatred for the war. Lots of people, not just me, go to him for advice.

I look for Jim in the usual places — the library, his dorm room, the Woodrow Wilson quadrangle — asking if anyone has seen him. Everywhere, he seems to have just left minutes before I arrive. Intent on finding him, I wear myself out, hopping from location to location.

Finally, after chasing him all Friday afternoon, I catch a glimpse of him briskly walking on the path toward lower campus.

"Jim," I call out, trot up to him, and say breathlessly, "I need to talk."

He stops as I grab his elbow, turning toward me. "I didn't see you last night in the chapel, Bruce. Were you there?" The war and protests are all he thinks about these days, so it's not surprising that this is how he greets me.

"I didn't go... for lots of reasons."

"These are not normal times." He's obviously irritated and disappointed in me. "We *have to* do something. We have to find some way to say, 'Stop!' You probably heard already that we're the first university to go on strike?"

"I know, Jim, but I don't know what that *means.*" I'm as bewildered as he is annoyed. "Everyone seems to think that a strike is the right response, but I'm not so sure. Exactly how does a strike hurt the national government?"

"Look, Bruce, a strike means a stoppage — a refusal to put up with intolerable conditions. Princeton, like a lot of universities, has a connection with the Pentagon. We provide the brains for the machine, and we need to say NO."

I'm sympathetic, but skeptical. "Are you talking about some kind of 'general strike' by all workers to shut down the government?" I ask. "Because I don't think it'll be easy to get those workers who beat up protestors to come around to our side. Nixon claims the 'silent major ity' stands with him."

I wonder... does Jim really believe that blue-collar workers who depend on Princeton to make a living — people like Cleve and Caddie — won't go to work because a bunch of pampered kids think it will make a difference in stopping the war?

Then I swallow hard and tell Jim what he already knows. "I'm also really afraid." I'd already heard that students at the chapel last night were turning in their draft cards. Some even burned them as a public statement of dissent. This seemingly harmless symbolic act carries enormous consequences: A 1965 law says that anyone who "knowingly destroys, knowingly mutilates" a draft card commits a criminal act, punishable by up to five years in prison and a $10,000 fine.

"I'm ashamed to say it," I add, "but I really can't afford to make one wrong step that could hurt my chances in San Diego."

He looks down, absorbing what I've said. When he gazes up at me again, I see compassion in his dark eyes. "I'm not going to sit in judgment of you, Bruce. You have a lousy number, and I don't. Sometimes I think my number has liberated me from the responsibilities you're shouldering."

Then he turns away, ready to keep moving. "But still, I need the Bruce Wasser I know to be at Jadwin on Monday," he says over his shoulder. "That's when students are planning to vote on a policy that defines the strike."

As Jim trots off to his next meeting, he glances back at me. "I'm depending on you, Bruce."

Over the weekend, the campus is like a disturbed beehive, buzzing with angry activity. All my friends are preparing for the meeting, making signs, debating proposals to discuss and vote on during Monday's meeting.

Standing on the sidelines, I wonder: Where is my moral strength? I'm strong in my conviction that I'm a true conscientious objector, but where are my principles when it comes to making a statement against

101

this war? Am I really a coward, afraid to take a risk to end this horrifying, expanding war?

I'm caught between Mary Ann Blaum and Martin Duberman. I hear Mary Ann warning me, loud and clear: "Don't get into any trouble with the law." At the same time, I hear Martin encouraging me to speak up and take a stand: "Others who love this nation have gone to jail for their beliefs."

Over the weekend I keep a low profile, occupying myself with as many shifts as I can get. Saturday night, when I'm finished with work, Cleve motions that he wants to talk with me, holding out as enticement a warm plate loaded with a rare treat: a large strip steak and a pile of salty French fries.

"My man," Cleve begins, as he takes a seat across from me at the kitchen table. "Somethin's going on with you. Come clean, now."

I set my plate on the table, take a seat, and start to cut up the steak. Then I look up from my plate at Cleve, marveling at how he always has a read on me. No point in dodging his question; he always finds a way to get me to talk.

"Cleve, I can't stop thinking about Monday's meeting at Jadwin. You're going, right?"

"Hell, yeah, man," Cleve says, clearly galvanized by the upcoming event. "But this ain't just about the war, you know. You gotta tie this thing with other issues." He pauses, looks around the kitchen, then continues. "You following what's going on at Yale?"

I know what Cleve is talking about. *The New York Times* had reported on a May Day protest, attended by an estimated 15,000 Yale students and others, on the New Haven Green. The New Haven event had attracted protesters from across the country to rally in support of the Black Panthers — a political organization dedicated to community organizing and "Black Power" — and to declare support for the liberation of Black people in the United States.

Cleve looks straight at me. "Wonder if anyone's gonna talk about the brothers on Monday. Ain't no escapin', Brucie boy... it's all tied up in one ugly bundle."

I stare at Cleve, realizing again that wherever I turn, things are interconnected. One issue bleeds into another, then into all the others.

"Cleve, I..." I stop talking and look down at my plate, the half-eaten food not nearly as appetizing as it was a few minutes ago. "I just don't know what to do."

"Hey, man!" Cleve stands, smiling broadly. "You think I got answers? Hell, I ain't even got the right questions."

* * *

After Nixon's speech, protests and riots erupt on campuses across the country. College students — mostly under the voting age of 21 — can't take their rage to the ballot box, so they're desperately searching for other ways to voice their objections: marches, sit-ins, and powerful individual gestures, such as turning in or burning draft cards.

Tricky Dick did buy himself some time with his cynical draft lottery; student protests quieted down for a few months. But the lull only draped a flimsy dressing over the gaping wound of the war. Now, Cambodia has ripped off the bandage and the scab underneath it, leaving American campuses bleeding and raw.

On Monday, more than 4,000 students, faculty, and community members pile into Jadwin Gymnasium, one of Princeton's newest buildings. The 250,000-square-foot multipurpose facility is the home court for the college's basketball team, but this afternoon the floor is set with thousands of chairs facing a platform erected as a stage for speakers. I search out a chair to join some of my Stevenson friends: Ric Singer, Mark Dare, Dave Brown, Maggie Schwarz.

"Welcome," the first speaker says as he steps to the microphone. "I have an important announcement." He stands silent, waiting for the rambunctious crowd to settle. Gradually, the buzzing audience quiets down.

"Some of you may have heard, but for those who haven't... just a half-hour ago, at 12:24 this afternoon, four college students —" his voice breaks, and he swallows to collect himself.

He starts again... "The Ohio National Guard fired on protesting students at Kent State University earlier today. They were at a rally opposing American involvement in Vietnam and, now, Cambodia.

"Four died," he says solemnly. "Nine are wounded."

Those who hadn't heard yet let out a collective gasp. I had caught the story on the radio, and now I scan the room to see how the news lands. Many are stunned; a few burst into tears; others look dazed, their eyes suddenly hollow. The war's latest casualties aren't overseas; they're a day's drive from here.

A murmur slowly builds throughout the gymnasium. Then the speaker hushes the audience. "A moment of silence, please, for the fallen protesters."

Jadwin falls silent; suddenly, we're sitting in a shrine. Everything has changed in those five words: Four died, nine are wounded. In this moment, we begin to realize the weight, the new risks, of what we are about to decide. The dead, the wounded, are now among us. Shock, sorrow and a fresh sense of urgency engulf the room.

Then, spontaneously, the chant rises: "Strike! Strike! Strike!" The energy in the room feels combustible.

As the noise dies down, before the next speaker steps up, we talk among ourselves about this bombshell news. The radio had reported only sketchy details on the Kent State killings, but all of us agree that the setting of the incident is a deep affront. Students were shot dead by soldiers on campus, a sanctuary of safety, democracy, and higher learning. To us, it's a heinous crime, committed in a place comparable to a house of worship.

"I can't help but think about King and Bobby, Medgar Evers and Malcolm." Dave, shaking his head in dismay, is speaking for the five of us. We're all on the left, in varying degrees, and we all adored these men. "We're slaying all our leaders — now, even our own students! There's no way to escape the violence. Who's next?"

At the podium, students present three proposals, up for debate. The first calls for Princeton to take a stand against the Cambodia invasion and devote all its resources and manpower to supporting that position. Academic work, including all classes, would come to a halt. A second, more left-wing proposal, supported by many members of SDS, likewise calls on the university to strike and, in addition, to sever its ties with the military Reserve Officers Training Corps (ROTC) program and the despised Institute of Defense Analysis (IDA), as well as to make a commitment to forgo all funding from the Department of Defense. The third proposal, from an "Anti-Strike Committee," proposes no change, urging the university to continue functioning as usual.

Remarkably, every person in Jadwin will be represented by an equal vote. An eminent tenured professor is no more important than a food-service worker. Graduating seniors don't outrank first-year students. Here, today, all voices, all votes carry the same weight.

The meeting stretches out over four hours as leaders pontificate and posture. Few speakers can resist the lure of thousands of upturned faces.

Students chant all kinds of slogans throughout the afternoon. At one point they boom, "Shut It Down to Open It Up," which, strangely, makes sense. Somehow, we need to puncture the insular bubble surrounding Princeton and join the national dialogue about the war.

Dave, who has keen political instincts, notices that few SDSers are in attendance. He suspects they all went up to Yale, in solidarity with the Black Panther protests.

In the end, the first proposal wins, with some 2,000 votes — a good 500 more than the more radical approach. The no-strike proposal only receives 180 votes. I support the first proposal. It's not that I disagree with the second proposal; I simply can't get behind any policy that SDS supports.

Princeton's vote to strike leaves many unanswered questions. With the university shutting down, what are my professors going to do about finals? Will the graduating seniors have a ceremony? There's talk of protesting the IDA; I worry what I'll do if my friends ask me to join them. What will I do when the campus goes on strike?

The next morning, the horror of yesterday's events sets in. *The Philadelphia Inquirer, The New York Times,* and other newspapers across the nation publish what will become an iconic photograph from the Kent State killings: A devastated protester kneels over a slain student, her mouth wide open in a cry of shock, panic and pain, the fingers on her right hand rigid, her arms outstretched as if beseeching God to intervene.

Instantly, she becomes the symbol of our anguish, trauma, and rage.

May 1970

What now?

That question haunts the entire campus after the strike vote. Normal academic activities have ceased: classes no longer meet; finals are postponed or canceled. Professors and students are trying, often together, to find a way forward that serves both conscience and necessity.

Below this urgently industrious surface, anger still seeps like lava, a molten rage that, sooner or later, will find a fissure. Meanwhile, organizations are bubbling up. The New Congress Movement induces some 500 of us to work for the election of anti-war candidates. More radical students, focusing on their antipathy toward the Selective Service System, form UNDO — the Union for Draft Opposition.

Despite the general disruption — and thankfully, for my finances as well as everyone's sustenance — the dining halls are still in operation. A couple of days after the strike vote, Ric and I meet as usual for breakfast. A smile plays on Ric's face as we take our seats.

"Well, Jerome, what are you going to do?"

"Buddy, I just don't know. I'm sure as hell not gonna get involved with anything SDS is doing."

"How about UNDO?" he asks, the smile still pulling at the corner of his mouth. Ric knows I won't do anything that could screw up my CO application. "Don't you think it's time to shit or get off the pot?"

"Ric, I... I've been thinking... maybe I should just go see my high school basketball coach next week and avoid the whole scene." I pause to get his reaction; he gazes at me impassively, waiting to see where this will go. "He's a vice principal now, and we write to each other every month or so. He'll be out here for a conference at West Point."

"West Point!" Ric bursts out laughing. "*West Point!* You gonna enlist while you're there?" Then he stops himself to needle me again "Yeah, that's right. Weren't you the star of your basketball team back then?"

He knows damn well that I was the 13th player on a 13-man team. I had to scrounge to get playing time in practice, and even that was a long shot. But Ric also knows I loved every minute of my time on the varsity team.

"Yeah, exactly, my man. I shattered every scoring record in San Diego County my senior year."

"Listen, Jerome. A lot of guys are demonstrating at the IDA. Why don't you go there and see if you can make a dent in the military-industrial complex?"

Ric is referring to the main focus of anti-war activity on campus. Some 1,000 protestors have marched on the Institute for Defense Analysis, starting what will become a five-day "siege." Some of my Stevenson friends are participating, but few are enthusiastic. The protest, they say, amounts to little more than organized chanting.

For me, it's not worth the risk. If I join a protest that's certain to be under police surveillance, I might as well take a blowtorch to my CO application.

Later in the day, I run into Jim, who has spent all day at the IDA protest. Though he knows I'm not about to get involved, he does seem enthusiastic about my going to West Point.

"Bruce, you have a good relationship with your coach, right? And he's pretty conservative, right? I mean, not a lot of lefties end up in school administration."

"Yeah," I reply skeptically. I've kept in touch with Eiler throughout my Princeton years, writing once or twice a month. But I've avoided discussing my attitudes about war, fearing that I would disappoint him.

"Just so you know," I tell Jim, "I don't get into politics with Coach when we write to each other."

"That's the point!" Jim jabs his left index finger at my chest. "You're going to see him in the belly of the beast, right? It's a perfect time to talk to him about the war... about your decision. Maybe even get him to reconsider his position. If you could change just one mind — his thinking — that would be a great contribution to the cause."

To tell the truth, I hadn't even thought of doing that — but what Jim says makes sense. Other than Martin Duberman, no adult male is more important to me than Coach Eiler.

I've known Coach since my first year in high school. (Clairemont comprised grades 10-11-12, like many American high schools at the time.) When Dad died, in January of that year, Eiler took me under his wing; then, during my junior and senior years, he found a place for me on the varsity basketball team. I respect — even revere — Coach Eiler. Now, a few years past my day-to-day relationship with him, I understand more clearly the important role he played in my life.

And I understand that facing him at this moment would actually require me to face myself in defending my beliefs. By going to West Point, I cannot only see Eiler again — my main goal — but also attempt to convert a "hawk" (as we called pro-war advocates) into a "dove." Changing even one mind is a start, and bringing Coach Eiler over to my viewpoint certainly would be more meaningful than anything I can hope to achieve on campus.

"Jim, what if he... if he...?" My voice catches, and I look down, unable to summon the courage to look him in the face.

"Bruce! What's the worst thing that could happen? He's not going to throw you out of his hotel window." He's trying to make me laugh, but clearly, he doesn't grasp how devastating it would be for me if I alienated Eiler.

"Jim, I think I'm going to need him to write a letter for me to the draft board. What if we get into it... and he thinks I'm some kind of freak? The kind of radical he hears about on the radio and TV?"

By now, many war supporters have bought into the stereotype of anti-war activists as a brainless herd of pot-smoking, flag-burning, America-hating hippies. I am none of these, but it *has* been a long time since Coach and I saw each other.

"Well, sometimes you have to face the music." Jim gives me a playful pat on the shoulder and pivots, heading toward the south end of campus, back to the IDA.

* * *

Several days later, I ask Professor Goldman if I might borrow his car to drive up to West Point. Over the past few months, he and his wife, Jo, have often offered me the use of their car. Whenever I've taken them up on it, I arrive to find that they've also generously provided some kind of sustenance: sometimes a couple of hot dogs, other times peanut butter and jelly sandwiches. The gesture suggests to me that not many undergraduates have taken the time to establish a relationship with this kind couple.

This time, knowing that Goldman, too, has become disillusioned with the war, I tell them where I'm going and what I hope to accomplish. Sure enough, when I pick up the car, I find on the front seat an Esso roadmap, neatly folded, with my route clearly marked. With these directions, I leave Princeton township and get on the Garden State Parkway with plenty of time to think about Coach and how I'll approach him.

I first met Richard C. "Dick" Eiler when he supervised an early morning PE class for athletes not playing sports in the fall. During a pick-up basketball game outdoors on asphalt courts, I dove for a ball going out of bounds. When Eiler saw my fearless drive, he called me over and asked me to try out for basketball that winter. I was hoping to become the catcher for the baseball team, but I tried out for basketball anyway.

The problem — then as now — was my complete lack of natural aptitude for basketball. I can't shoot; I have no off-hand dribbling skills; I'm not even all that tall. No doubt, more than 100 guys could have beaten me one-on-one. But, in that single dive for the ball, Coach Eiler saw what my father had instilled in me: a desire to work hard and help the team.

At the onset of the season, Eiler, as varsity coach, had almost no contact with me. As a player of little talent or promise, I languished on the JV bench. The only time my dad saw me play in a game was during an intra-squad match.

By that time, cancer had ravaged Joe's body, and he was a shell of his former self. I remember looking across the court at him; he was sitting alone, huddled in the top row of the stands. His face was gray, his shoulders stooped. The few minutes I spent on the court were utterly unmemorable, and when I returned to my spot at the end of the bench, I burned with embarrassment. I'd played horribly, and I began to wonder why Coach Eiler had wanted me to try out in the first place.

One month later, Dad was dead. Before I left school to accompany my family to Seattle, where Dad would be buried, Coach Eiler called me into his office. There, on top of a filing cabinet, an array of photos depicted a younger Eiler during his years as a star player at the University of Utah. Alongside the action shots stood a recent photo of Eiler with his family. The wall behind his desk held plaques honoring his many achievements.

He rose from his chair and scanned me, from my size 11 ½ basketball shoes to my crew-cut hair. "Bruce, I know how close you were to your father. I'm still close to mine." Then, looking directly at me, he said, as if reading my mind: "You didn't cause his illness, Bruce. None of this is your fault."

Immediately, words tumbled out. "Coach, I'm awful at basketball. Everyone knows it. My friends even count how many lay-ups I make before the game, because they know I'll never play —"

I felt the ground opening up beneath me, as if I were losing my balance, but I had to ask: "Coach — do you still want me on the team?"

"Listen, young man," he answered firmly, "there will always be a place for you in this program. Let me make those decisions. I have my reasons." I had no idea what these were — but they certainly didn't include my free-throw ability.

"Now," Eiler said, with the natural authority of a good coach, "take care of yourself. Take as much time away from the team as you need before you return. Your mother and sisters will need you now, more than ever." He took my hand, his palm engulfing mine, and reassuringly administered a solid handshake.

Now, in faraway New Jersey, the Hudson River winds on my right as I drive north, heading into New York. After the long, barren Princeton winter, it's nice to see the trees leafing out in early spring green.

The closer I get to West Point, the more Coach Eiler becomes my companion in the car. I can hear his voice, see his gestures, feel his presence. When I was on the varsity team, my junior and senior years, Eiler wasn't much older than his players. At six-foot-three, he carried his weight on a powerful frame; incipient middle age hadn't yet softened his physique. To me, he epitomized athletic masculinity: strong, handsome, understated.

During games, Coach Eiler invariably wore a blue blazer with gray slacks. He parted his closely cropped dark hair on the left side, leaving his rectangular face open to register a range of emotions. For a big man, Coach had a remarkably small voice, but he didn't need anything more. His team worshiped him.

A devout member of the Church of Latter-Day Saints, Eiler lived in the same middle-class neighborhood as my family. On weekends, I often spent time with his family, and his wife, Jan, made sure I never left their home on an empty stomach. Our senior yearbook carried a full-page spread on Eiler, with a photograph and his quote: "I try to teach the sacred aspects of basketball." His coaching philosophy was to play for each other; put the team above individual needs; respectfully represent your school.

For two years, practices became my games. I wasn't on the floor much, so I wanted to find another way to make a contribution — and it came through books. After researching a variety of defenses at the local library, I would go to Coach's house to talk strategies with him. During games — especially when we were on the road, visiting raucous competitors — my job was to protect Eiler's ever-present bottle of milk, which he stashed under his chair, reaching for regular sips to calm a perpetually upset stomach.

We "scrub-inis" knew that our role was to cheerlead and provide information to those on the floor. I never felt I was "riding the pine"; rather, I gave full voice to my father's sports philosophy, that the lines on the floor were irrelevant. All of us were in the game at every moment, shouting out screens, calling out the other team's predictable plays. At game's end, my uniform was as sweaty and drenched as those of the players on the court.

For my "play," Eiler selected me twice as "Most Inspirational Player," an honor previously unheard of. At our senior banquet, Coach Eiler paid me the highest athletic compliment I've ever received: "I've coached many fine players in my time, but if I had to start a team from scratch, the first person I'd pick would be Bruce Wasser."

Only now, barely into my twenties, was I beginning to see why he had kept me on his squad. Maybe he saw me as the heart of the team; maybe he'd had other reasons. Regardless, it would kill me to disappoint him.

* * *

I pull into the parking lot of the huge old Thayer Hotel at West Point, step out of the Goldmans' car, and stretch my legs, taking in the commanding views of the Hudson River and the United States Military Academy. Butterflies flit in my stomach, but I don't have a bottle of milk — for Eiler or for me.

Walking into the Thayer's grand lobby, I stare up at the soaring ceilings, arched stained-glass windows, antique chandeliers, and dark wainscoting. When I spot Coach leaning against a white column, waiting for me, my stomach drops and my heart steps up into full pounding.

Eiler looks older, more relaxed and at ease with himself than I recall. He's put on a few pounds, and his hair is graying at the temples. Otherwise, he's still characteristically "Coach."

My eyes fall upon the lapel pin on his navy-blue sports jacket — a gold-trimmed American flag. In my world, very few people sport one of these. He looks like he belongs here, in this militaristic setting. And the pin — a badge of his conservatism — reminds me of exactly what I'm up against.

He nods, reaches out to shake my hand, and holds it longer than necessary, all while giving me a thorough once-over. "You look different from your days at CHS, Bruce," he says, with both a smile and a grimace. I smile, too, but nervously, as I try to flatten my unruly hair while glancing down at my student clothes. My scruffy college look must be quite a surprise — and I definitely *don't* fit in here, not at all.

We settle into two upholstered chairs, their straight backs as dignified as the elegant lobby. Only then do I notice more of the hotel's decor: US flags standing in the corners, plaques celebrating war heroes, portraits of military leaders adorning the lobby's walls.

How ironic to have this difficult conversation about war in a quiet, beautiful place dedicated to celebrating 200 years of American military history. This, Jim, truly is "the belly of the beast."

We start by catching up: chatting about players on the 1966 and 1967 teams, what we've been doing since we both left Clairemont High, how our families are doing. Eiler tells me he feels he's found his calling as a school administrator. He's here to attend a conference with colleagues from across the country.

An awkward silence descends upon us as we exhaust the small talk. I wonder how I can start a discussion about his position on the war. Then I hit on a segue to approach the topic.

"Coach, you know we went on strike last week at Princeton," I say tentatively.

"Yes, I'm aware," he says, with a grimace. "Most campuses are on strike now, I guess."

"Well, I didn't feel good about any of the protests on campus," I'm hoping this will let me open up our conversation.

"I'm glad to hear that!" Visibly relieved, he cracks a smile. "I always knew you had your head on straight."

"Uh, I don't think you understand." I jump in, quick to correct his thinking. "Maybe you don't know... I've applied to be a conscientious objector."

Clearly, he didn't know; his shoulders sag as he absorbs this blow. Shaking his head, he says softly, "That's *not* the young man I knew in high school."

"I... I know you don't agree with me." I try to look him in the eye, but he's gazing off, as if he's staring at the kid sitting on the bench, wearing too-tight bottoms. As the 13th player, I got the only uniform left — an extra-small. In the locker room, my teammates would time me to see how long it took to squeeze into my shorts.

I press on. "But I want to stop this war and, instead of protesting, I thought maybe it would help if I could change one person's mind about Vietnam. So, I... I'd like to talk to you about your position. I know how much you support the president and how much you care about America —"

"Listen, young man," he bristles, his tone a mixture of anger and paternity. He's already shaking a finger at me, as if he were reprimanding me back in high school. "I know you. But I don't know why you've made this decision."

"C... Coach —" My voice cracks as I try to gather my thoughts.

"You would turn your back on the country that has done so much for you?" Eiler talks right over me, obviously as passionate about the war as I am. "I see young people in the streets, spitting on the flag, burning their draft cards. It makes me sick."

Sitting through this won't be easy, I think. But I tell myself, I've stood up to my mother, and I can do it here.

"Coach. After Dad died," I say, trying to steady myself, "something... sort of... *broke* inside of me. Then, after Martin and Bobby were murdered, I knew that I could never go to war. I know that other guys applying for CO status have other motivations. My reason comes from a broken heart and a commitment to non-violence."

"Look, Number 11," he says — and, suddenly, I'm 17 years old again, sitting on the bench, smelling the sweat and hearing the cheers from the stands. Only Eiler has ever called me "Number 11."

What he doesn't understand is that I'm not 17 anymore. I'm 21 years old, and a different number – 90 — now defines and drives me.

"It makes me sad to hear you talk this way. All of us have sorrows and pain, but that's no reason to turn your back on America." Eiler pauses, his steely, gray-eyed gaze burns me, and I see his recalcitrance in it. "When you were on my team, I knew exactly what to expect of you.

"You, more than anyone else, knew what it meant to sacrifice for others," he says, as if he's rallying our squad in the locker room. "You always put team above anything else. You never gave in to selfishness, and you always gave me unqualified support, even when I made decisions that confused or upset you.

"That's exactly what your country is asking of you now." Eiler hammers home his point. "You may not like the president; you may hate the war. But a patriot never questions authority. He does what's asked of him, without reservations —"

"Coach —" I interrupt him, trying hard not to sound as nervous as I feel. "I love this country, but it's ruining itself. Seems to me, a good patriot *always* questions what's right or wrong. I had hoped you would see the cost of this war, that it's not winnable. It's not right."

He shakes his head in disgust. "Bruce, I don't know what's happened to you." He points to my faded Princeton sweatshirt, well-worn jeans, disheveled hair. "Of all the boys on the team, I thought better of you. I thought you would do what your country asks.

"I talked to your father when he was dying. We discussed our backgrounds, our histories." I flash on the one game Dad attended; now I remember that, after it was over, he and Eiler had an intense conversation on the side of the court. I wondered what they could be talking about that was so serious.

Then it hits me: Maybe in that last conversation, Dad told Eiler he was dying and asked Coach to take care of me. If Eiler agreed — and he surely would have — that explains why he kept me on the team. Now, I feel even more chagrined and humiliated.

"He was very proud of his military record," Eiler goes on. "It hurts me to say this, Bruce."

Coach pauses, dropping his gaze to his lap, as if he's debating with himself whether he should go on. Then he raises his eyes, looks at me straight on, and says what he's thinking.

"No father could have been prouder of his son than he was, but your dad would be worried about you now. He wouldn't agree with you. I doubt you would have changed his mind on the war, and you won't change mine, either."

Another strained silence divides us, and we both shift uncomfortably in our chairs. "Coach," I say softly after some time, "thanks for listening to me. I don't know if you realize, but I still play ball almost every day, and I think of you every time I step on a court. I'm sorry I've disappointed you."

"You can always change your mind, Bruce. America is calling, and she needs the 'Most Inspirational' people on her side."

That cuts deep, but I clench my teeth and tell myself to hold my ground.

"You're too good a man to abandon our country and this place," Eiler adds with a flourish, spreading his arms wide to encompass the martial spirit of West Point and the grand Thayer Hotel.

"I have to listen to my own heart," I say slowly to my coach, surprised to hear how confident I sound. Then, to underscore my conviction, I add, "Even when it hurts those I admire most."

"Promise me, Bruce, you'll think about what I've said. Keep in touch with me. Don't stop writing letters to me."

"Coach, I hope you'll keep an open mind, too."

Forcing a smile — even though my heart is in my stomach — I manage to lighten the tone.

"And maybe one day, you'll even replace that flag pin on your lapel with a peace button." I can't believe I said that.

Then I beam at this man I love. "It would be my privilege to send you one."

SUMMER - EARLY FALL 1970

Back in San Diego for the summer, even before unpacking my suitcase, I retrace my path to the draft board office. I've got to tell Mary Ann Blaum that I can't count on Coach Eiler for a letter of reference. I had hoped Eiler would serve as the keystone of my CO application by attesting to my character, but my West Point visit proved otherwise.

As I push open the door, I notice that Mary Ann has changed the style of her glasses, from John Lennon granny glasses to dark-gray aviators. She's on the phone and points to a chair, silently telling me to take a seat while she finishes her call.

"We need *duplicate* copies," she says firmly into the phone, as I sit down and look around her small office. Having grown accustomed to this place, I'm much less intimidated by Tricky Dick's severe countenance and beady eyes. As expected, I hear the familiar din of constantly ringing phones, along with the rhythmic clunk-and-swish of the hulking Xerox machines in the next room. Summer has added the steady hum of the air-conditioning window unit.

After she returns the receiver to its cradle, Mary Ann gently pushes a stack of files to the side of her desk, leans on her elbows, and takes a long, friendly look at me. "Well, Bruce, what brings you here?"

"Mary Ann." I sound anxious already — but then, I sound anxious every time I come here, so that's how she knows me. How is she going to react to my fiasco with Coach Eiler? Would it be better if I didn't mention it? Is there anyone who knows me as well as Eiler who can give me a positive character reference?

Halting the debate that has been pounding through my head for days now, I blurt out, "I need to talk with you about something that happened a few weeks ago." I figure I should tell her the whole story, so I start by saying, "You know that Princeton went on strike, right?"

"I don't know what's wrong with you students," she snaps, erasing the warmth that had brightened her face. "Here you have a chance to get a great education, and you decide you don't want it? How do you think that makes those of us who never had that chance feel?"

Worry tinges her voice as her eyes narrow. "Wait a minute — strike! You weren't part of that, were you? You didn't get into trouble?"

"No, no, everything's okay, Mary Ann." I try to sound reassuring. "I did *vote* to go on strike, but I didn't participate in the campus protests. I did something else."

Shifting in my uncomfortable chair, I say, "But before I get to that, I need to straighten something out, Mary Ann. I don't want you to think I don't care about my education. I care a lot! All my coursework is in good standing."

"Something else?" Her eyebrows arch in alarm. "What did you do?"

"Remember, I told you that I hoped my high-school basketball coach would write a letter for me..."

"Yes," she nods slowly. "He sounded ideal."

"Yeah, well, that's not going to work out." I shake my head for emphasis. "Not happening!"

"Why not?"

"I went to meet with him when he was at a conference in West Point." I explain that it had been years since I last saw him. "I know he supports the war," I say, "and I thought, instead of protesting, I could try to change one person's mind — his."

"And...?"

"It didn't go well," I shake my head again. "He didn't budge. And, after our conversation, he's probably even more committed to supporting the war. He didn't like the way I look —" I point in the direction of my long hair and bushy sideburns — "and he didn't like anything I had to say.

"What's worse," I confess, "he told me that he's disappointed in me." My voice trails off, and I drop my head so Mary Ann won't see my shame. "He knew my father, and he said Dad would have been just as upset, just as disappointed."

Taking a deep breath, I finally deliver the worst of it. "He even questioned my patriotism. That's when I knew I couldn't ask him for a letter."

Mary Ann sighs, removes her glasses, and rubs her nose on the twin red spots where they rest. "Look, Bruce, what did you expect?" She wipes the lenses on her skirt and shakes them a little, as if to toss off any remaining lint. Then she returns her glasses to her nose.

"Did you really think some scruffy-looking former basketball player could waltz into West Point and make a case against the war, and the heavens would open up and alter this man's long-standing political views?"

When she puts it that way, I'm ashamed that my plan sounds so foolish. "I wanted to do *something* to change things," I pipe up defensively. From Mary Ann's perspective, however, I must seem incredibly naive.

"Wait... and you did this at West Point?" She shakes her head in utter disbelief.

"Well," she then concedes, "better than protesting, I suppose."

She contemplates my situation for a moment, then surprises me.

"Don't give up on your coach, Bruce. From what you've told me, it sounds like he has a lot of respect for you. In fact, a letter from him would probably be the most important one we receive."

I'm skeptical. If he writes what he said to me, my CO application is sunk. I can see the letter already, riddled with words like "disingenuous," "disillusioned," "disloyal."

"His letter *would* be against the grain," she continues to make her case. "Most people you ask to write on your behalf probably don't like the war and sympathize with your claim. But he isn't writing about the war, Bruce. He's writing about *you*."

Maybe, I think — maybe Mary Ann is right. I doubt that Coach Eiler would ever undermine me. Certainly not behind my back. And he wouldn't violate his notion of the meaning of "team" — even if he believes I've dishonored that pledge.

"OK, Mary Ann, I'll call him and ask for a character reference," I say. "But maybe I'll hold off until next spring. I hope, by then, he'll change his mind about the war."

"I'm guessing," Mary Ann replies with an encouraging smile, "he'll come through for you."

* * *

During the summer, I'm at home as little as possible. I find happiness and solace through my old Clairemont High friends, some of whom are still living in San Diego – including my girlfriend, whom my mother still can't stand. Weekdays I'm at work, serving as an activity director for an after-school program at Gompers Junior High, a predominantly African American school in east San Diego. My salary comes from Princeton University's "Summer in the Cities" program, which pays scholarship students like me to work in communities plagued by poverty and discrimination.

Between work and my girlfriend, I'm able to limit my contact with my mother. Mom and I have established an uneasy truce about my CO application — a tense silence that's certainly an improvement over fighting, but I wouldn't call it peace. Rather, it amounts to a policy of "don't ask, don't tell."

But this approach fosters a deep, sad sense of alienation. All day, every day, I feel the aching void of not having a parent who is capable of listening to me.

I also find myself increasingly worried about my youngest sister, Cindy. At 14, she has climbed out of childhood and now is pounding on the door of adolescence. She's growing into her adult body, and boys are taking an acute interest in her. Mom has told me that Cindy doesn't like school, and it's easy to see why: her inability to focus in the classroom has resulted in dismal grades and numerous referrals to the school's behavioral authorities. She smokes whenever she can get her hands on a cigarette, and it would be foolish to assume that she hasn't moved on to alcohol and drugs.

In the house, we still don't talk much about Dad's death, but his absence hangs like a heavy shroud over our family. Conversations never go beyond the business of the day — who needs a ride, where they're going, what time is dinner. My mother and sisters, it seems, are barely getting by; each of us is sequestered in our own world of pain.

I find relief from my own unspoken sadness at the beach. San Diego's beaches epitomize the beauty and sun-splashed image of Southern California; they have the power to soothe, even for a guy who can't surf. The enormity of the ocean puts my own hurts in some perspective. Even getting there calms me, partly because I enjoy driving by Jack Murphy Stadium, where the Padres play.

One sweltering Saturday in June, I decide to do something I haven't done in years: attend a major-league baseball game. In high school, I loved seeing the minor-league San Diego Padres play in the old Westgate Park. Our chemistry teacher, Mr. McKinstry, worked in the box office during the summers, and he invariably found ways to slip us a few tickets.

In 1969, when the Padres became a National League expansion team, they moved several miles east, into the cavernous Jack Murphy Stadium. Like most expansion teams, the Padres were terrible, losing more than 100 games in their first season. By 1970, another disastrous season, the glamor of having our own major-league team had faded, and it wasn't hard to get good seats.

After Dad died, going to a baseball game was never again a simple pleasure for me. Win or lose, the experience was bittersweet, evenly divided between my love and appreciation for the game and my deep sense of loss — as big as the stadium itself. In my heart and my mind, the sport was bound up with Dad.

As my coach throughout my Little League years, Dad insisted that his players call him "Skip," on the basis of his belief that the title "coach" was reserved for football and basketball. Skip made me a catcher, instructing me to employ "the tools of ignorance." A major leaguer in the 1930s, Herold "Muddy" Ruel, had coined this term to describe what it takes to be a catcher: the intelligence to be effective behind the plate, and the idiocy to play in a position that requires so much safety equipment. Dad sensed that I had this rare blend of intelligence and idiocy, and he was right. I proudly wore Number 8 — same as my idol, Yogi Berra.

Dad spent countless hours on the mound throwing to me, teaching me — as a catcher — to see the spin on the ball, and showing me how to use my hips and legs to increase bat speed as a hitter. In his coaching, Skip stressed the mental aspects of the game. Often, he'd turn to one of his players on the bench and pointedly ask: "What's the count?

126

How many outs? What did the batter do last time up?" We knew he expected us to have the right answers.

Skip saw baseball in the context of its place in American culture. Success in baseball depends upon individual excellence and team cooperation. For years, it was an avenue for immigrants and, belatedly, African-Americans to incorporate themselves into larger society. My father never spoke of anti-Semitism, but I believe he saw sports — particularly baseball — as a way to lay claim to being American, on a par with everyone else.

He taught me the history of baseball, telling me stories of ballplayers from the 1930s and '40s, when he was growing up. We never missed watching the "Game of the Week" on our black-and-white TV, devoutly listening to Dizzy Dean and Pee Wee Reese talk ball on their Saturday show. I copied Dad and Diz, mastering a melodic whistling version of "The Wabash Cannonball" — the song Diz performed when a game lagged.

One evening in Seattle, when I was 12, Dad took me to a Pacific Coast League Rainiers game at Sick's Stadium. Johnny Pesky was the Rainiers' manager, and several loudmouths sitting behind us heckled him mercilessly for supposedly having cost the Red Sox the World Series back in 1946. Baiting the diminutive former shortstop, they accused him of freezing at a crucial seventh-inning moment in the deciding game of the Series.

"Hey, Needle Nose, how much longer you gonna hold the ball?" one taunter yelled, howling with laughter at his own joke. His sidekicks called Pesky a "busher" and a "choker."

Dad leaned over to me and quietly explained that Pesky had unselfishly, undeservedly, shouldered blame for losing the game, never once deflecting the criticism onto his teammates. To my father, the Rainiers' skipper modeled every virtue of the game we so loved.

As the hecklers tossed one insult after another, I looked sideways at Dad and noticed his jaw muscles clenching in a familiar dance of anger. He listened, seething. Finally, unable to tolerate their ignorant blather, he rose from his seat — his six-foot-two frame towering as he stood — and turned around to face the men.

Fifteen years after he stopped playing pro football, Dad still looked formidable. His sandy hair — thinning now, no longer curly — topped a rugged, trapezoidal face. When he was provoked, his green eyes narrowed and his nostrils flared. At this moment, all the warnings of incipient rage were flashing.

"You fatheads don't know shit from Shinola," he barked at the startled men. "Pesky was a fine ballplayer then, and he never — not once — complained about the abuse fools like you threw at him. Now, shut up."

Then Dad sat back down. They didn't say another word.

I identified with Dad in so many ways and, sadly, I suffered the same loss he did, at exactly the same age. Dad's father also died at 42, when Dad, too, was only 15. His death left my Grandma Alice penniless. The family lived in Atlanta then, and Grandma Alice packed up herself and her children – Joe and his younger sister, Eileen — and relocated to the first public-housing development built during the New Deal, in Techwood, near Georgia Tech University. After graduating from Marist High School, where he lettered in four sports, Joe attended Tech.

Following World War II, Joe played for the Seattle-Tacoma Indians, a minor-league pro football team in the Pacific Coast League. There, the Detroit Lions scouted and signed him — but before his first big-league season began, an injury sidelined him. Idled, he realized that this might be only the first of many injuries. It was a moment to decide between two futures: staying in a sport that could ruin his health, or giving up football to marry the woman he loved. His choice led directly to my existence.

Now, all these years later, I'm almost as tall as Dad was, and happily making my way to my seat down the third-base line. I whistle "The Wabash Cannonball" as I watch infield and batting practice for the hour before the game — something Dad and I always did. Fans slowly file in, and I wince when I notice a group of middle-aged men, all outfitted in shirts bearing the Padres' white, brown and gold colors, shuffling to the seats right behind me. Long before the game begins, they're already drunk and toting even more beers.

The public-address announcer reads the starting line-ups, then intones: "Ladies and gentlemen, to honor America and our armed forces, please rise for our national anthem."

I've always loved "The Star-Spangled Banner" — but today, something tells me not to stand. It doesn't feel right to publicly pledge myself to a country so divided and derailed. Instead, I simply stay seated, bowing my head and softly whistling the melody.

"Hey! Looka this!" One of the drunks behind me is already slurring his words. "Asshole thinks he's too good to stand. Fuckin' fag."

"Fuckin' no-good freak," his buddy chimes in. "Probably a draft dodger, from the looks of 'im."

When the song reaches "the bombs bursting in air," the third guy lets loose with a "bomb" of his own — dumping his large cup of beer over my head.

"That'll teach this fucker!" he hollers. "If he doesn't like America, then he oughta leave it."

My body stiffens with humiliation; rage surges through me, and I can feel my jaw muscles pulsating. After the last note of the anthem, I stand, my hair dripping with beer, my T-shirt soaked and sticking to my skin. Slowly, I turn around and glare, drilling into each of them, roping one to the next.

Then I make my way to the aisle, edging past seated fans as the men continue to mock me. "Look at that fuckin' pussy," one yells. "He's going somewhere to cry." Howling laughter follows me as I climb the stairs to the concessions area.

Not one person comes to my defense. No one even looks at me.

I find a stadium representative and describe what happened. I'm shaking with fury, but I manage to speak calmly and deliberately.

"Here's the deal, either you kick them out of the stadium, or I'm going to call the police and have them charged with battery."

The rep listens, silent and impassive. Maybe he won't do anything. That would be just as violating as the perpetrators' mockery.

"There are plenty of witnesses," I continue, trying to impress upon him that I mean business. "I don't care what you think of my not standing for the anthem. But I have the right to protest, and you can't allow them to get away with open, blatant cruelty in the baseball stadium."

The representative tells me to wait while he gets his supervisor. Ten minutes later, in the bottom of the first inning, the supervisor appears, listens to my story, and goes to remove the men.

As I return to my seat, I glare at the bystanders, silently rebuking them for their inaction. The seats behind mine are empty now. Looking around the stadium, I wonder if the men were actually kicked out or if the supervisor just sent them to sit elsewhere. No matter, I tell myself, I stood my ground — and acted on my beliefs — during the anthem. And even though I was bullied, I didn't give up my seat or leave the game.

In a few innings, the hot sun has dried my hair and shirt, and I've calmed down enough to enjoy the game. During the seventh-inning stretch, when the crowd rises and boisterously sings "Take Me Out to the Ballgame," I enthusiastically rise from my seat and sing the words of baseball's iconic song.

After all, my father would never forgive me if I disrespected the game.

FALL 1970

As my senior year begins, the campus is back to normal; many juniors and seniors behave as if the tumultuous events of last spring never happened. This year, I'm living in a single room, enjoying the solitude — until one morning in early October.

Awake and ready to jump out of bed, I discover instead that I can barely move. Alone and frightened, I manage to call Ric, who rushes over and half-walks, half-drags me to the campus infirmary.

There, I mostly doze off as the nurses and on-call doctor perform a series of tests. After examining the results of my bloodwork, the doctor delivers my diagnosis: a mild but serious case of meningitis.

"It's a good thing you came in when you did, Bruce," he says somberly. "You're going to need to rest. No school for a week, maybe ten days."

"Ten days!" Snapping back to consciousness, I'm more panicked about my classes and work schedule than my health. "I need to work on my thesis! How can I let my professors know why I'm absent?"

"Whoa," the doctor gently rebukes me. "We'll let your professors know. I'll also have the staff call your mother."

"My *mother?*" Now I'm aghast. "Do you have to?"

Although I'm 21 years old, I don't have the right to control my own medical information, and the university feels an obligation to inform my family. I'm relieved the doctors will let my professors know why I'm not in class, but I'm instantly in knots knowing that Mom will get this information.

But events and days run together while I'm laid up in the infirmary. Weakened and addled by fever, I can't keep things straight. I know that Jim, Ric, and other friends are visiting me; Garvey and Martin come by, and the Goldmans send flowers. One oddly vivid experience is my first encounter with cream of mushroom soup: I'm immediately, memorably revolted by its texture and taste.

In the afternoons, I watch the World Series between the Baltimore Orioles and the Cincinnati Reds on television. Almost nothing registers in my foggy brain, except that one of the umpires is Emmett Ashford, the first African American to work all five games in the Series. I have a sweet memory of Dad and me together, watching him ump a game in the Pacific Coast League, back in Seattle.

One night, the nurses connect my room phone to a long-distance call. My mother's shrill voice pierces the infirmary quiet as she wastes no time in getting to the point.

"This is great news, Bruce. Don't you see?"

"Great news?" I ask groggily. That's the last thing I expected her to say, but her staccato cadence tells me that she thinks she's sharing something exciting.

"I've been on the phone with Dr. Fish," she explains, reveling in her own importance, "and he says he can get you out of the draft now. You can get a medical exemption!"

She pauses, waiting for my response. Now, I'm wide awake and simmering mad, but I don't say anything.

"Bruce, aren't you happy? Now you can go to law school. You can forget about this *mishigas* with the war. This may be the best thing that ever happened to you —"

"Mom!" Interrupting, I try to stop her runaway train. "Mom, aren't you going to even ask how I am?" I'm shocked by her lack of concern, but even more stung that she has violated the detente we reached, only weeks ago, about her not interfering with my CO application.

"Of course, I'm concerned about you. I'm your mother, in case you've forgotten," she says, and then justifies her cheeriness. "But I spoke with the doctor there, and he said there's nothing to worry about. Naturally, I know you're in good hands."

"Mom, that's not the issue." I try to steer the conversation away from my CO application. "I wish the university hadn't called you about this."

"Dr. Fish is writing a letter right now." She doesn't miss a beat. "He's going to mail it to me..."

"Mom!" I yell into the receiver, unable to stop her — or myself. "I need to do this my own way. Don't you *dare* send that letter to the draft board!"

A nurse pokes her head in the door to see what's going on. I wave her off, relieved that, finally, Mom is stunned into silence.

"I'm not asking you." I lower my voice and continue firmly. "If you go behind my back on this, I don't know... I don't know what I'll do. Promise me! *Promise me!*"

She says nothing; there will be no promises. Once again, we're standing on opposite sides of an abyss that grows wider with each fight. My furious silence lets her know that she's on the precipice of losing me altogether.

That forces her to concede. "Okay. *Okay,* but you're making a big mistake!" But she can't give me a full victory; instead, she finds a way to undercut my demand and save face. "I'll get the letter and hold onto it, just in case you come to your senses."

"Mom, I know I'm disappointing you." Flopped back down on my pillow, I'm barely able to speak above a whisper.

"I just don't know what's gotten into you, Bruce." Even at this distance, I can see her roll her eyes, shake her head, throw up her hands in exasperation. "You were such a good kid. Now... I just don't know."

"You have to let me be my own man," I tell her again.

We say a cold, tense goodbye. As I set down the receiver, I realize she never *did* ask me how I'm feeling.

* * *

After recovering from meningitis, I spend much of October completing applications to law schools — despite the grim reality that I could be drafted before my first semester. Still, doing my best to stay focused on the future, I patiently fill out one form after another in my neatest handwriting.

Most of my friends are applying to prestigious Ivy League law schools, but I have no desire to spend any more time on the East Coast. Instead, I concentrate on my top three choices, all in the San Francisco Bay area: Stanford, Boalt Hall (at UC Berkeley), and Santa Clara Law School.

For years, I've wanted to be a criminal defense attorney. My ambition was sparked in the most American way: a popular television series of the early 1960s, "The Defenders," introduced me to the profession. The show, framed by a dramatic theme song trumpeting justice, starred the venerable E. G. Marshall and Robert Reed as a father-son legal team. The pair was presented as altruistic servants of the law — perfect for a boy yearning to make a difference in the world. I much preferred their dignified style of advocacy over the more popular but, in my opinion, distastefully flashy Perry Mason, whose smug talents I considered better suited to shady plots and private investigators than serious legal work.

However, a real-life attorney had an even greater influence on me than my favorite TV series. During seventh grade, I attended Sunday school at Temple de Hirsch, where Murray Guterson, one of Seattle's most famous and feared criminal defense attorneys, was my teacher.

It was a rare man who could make a baseball-crazed 12-year-old jump out of bed at 7 a.m. on a Sunday to go to religious school. Guterson was that man — so engaging that, to my mother's amazement, I never argued about going to his class.

And it wasn't just me. Guterson had an amazing ability to grab and hold the attention of 20 fidgety kids on the verge of adolescence. We sat in awe as he guided us through the study of Jewish ethics. Using the Socratic method of dialogue and debate, he taught us to draw equally on logic and passion as we argued about civil rights, point-shaving sports scandals, and Jewish resistance during the Holocaust. He showed us how the law was the best avenue to change the world — to make whole what's broken in society. He was so compelling, so inspiring, that I wanted to *be* Murray Guterson when I grew up.

But now, as I work my way toward that life path, the LSAT – Law School Aptitude Test – douses the fire Guterson ignited. I've never done well on standardized tests. Now, even as I'm taking the LSAT, I'm anxious that my scores will mirror my unimpressive SATs.

Weeks pass before the LSAT results trickle in through the agonizingly slow mail. Seniors immediately compare their scores and — being Princetonians – compete over this new standard of measurement. "What did you get on the LSAT?" replaces the previously ubiquitous "What's your lottery number?"

When I receive my own LSAT scores, the mediocre results instantly confirm my apprehension. For me, numbers have turned into footmen for the gods of fate. Most of my friends not only have lottery numbers better than mine; now they have higher LSAT scores, too.

April is a long time away, but I fear the envelopes I'll receive will be thin.

In November, I face a different challenge — one arising from Martin's experimental course on American radicalism. By this point in his teaching career, Martin is through with traditional techniques. He despises the sterile intellectualism that pervades Princeton's fabled preceptorials: small discussion classes in which students duel each other for the professor's attention. Far from inspiring thoughtful, creative analysis, these groups often devolve into a frantic contest, with everyone racing to identify and promote the right answer — the professor's favored concept, or "key 'cept." The goal is to best and impress all present.

Martin's conception for the American radicalism course is not only the exploration of theories and practices of radicalism, but also the guiding principle of the class itself. Banishing traditional education entirely, he eliminates required readings, written assignments, and even lectures, preferring to experiment with innovative teaching techniques. This approach places responsibility for learning on students, who, Martin believes, will respond by bringing passion to their inquiry into the subject.

For most of the semester, I focus on American anarchists of the late nineteenth and early twentieth centuries. The complicated, perplexing Emma Goldman intrigues and challenges me most, with her disdain for authority and bold claim to her absolute right to control her own destiny — as a philosopher, a Jew, a woman, and a human being.

Often, I find myself writing about my own differences from "Red Emma," as I contemplate the depth and sincerity of my own beliefs and my fear of going to prison. Goldman was imprisoned several times throughout her life for "inciting to riot," illegally distributing information about birth control, and conspiring to "induce persons not to register" for the newly instated draft in 1917.

Toward the end of the semester, Martin firmly rebukes Princeton's customary methods by announcing that our class is about to engage in an "encounter group." Our engagement with radicalism, he says, demands more than passion. He now wants his students to "go deeper" than any professor in any preceptorial has ever imagined: to rip off our protective, defensive outer shells and reveal what's roiling inside us.

Martin explains that he is bringing in a psychologist who is trained to lead such groups. Under his guidance, participants strip away their veneers and pretenses, thereby increasing self-awareness and eliciting greater sensitivity to others. By admitting and addressing our worries and fears — by being "authentic" — he believes we can grow closer to each other and attain a better understanding of ourselves.

I have never heard of any of this.

One Thursday evening, fifteen of us take over one of the small rooms upstairs in Stevenson Hall for this special event. Most of the students flop onto the worn sofas, but I'm too apprehensive to get comfortable. Instead, I plant myself on the floor, right near the door, in case I need to bail out fast.

When the dark-haired, bearded psychologist steps up to introduce himself to the group, he speaks with confidence and authority. "I'm a trained leader, here to help maintain a safe, intimate, and meaningful atmosphere," he explains. "Here, you're free to express yourself and experiment in new ways. You will find you can change your behavior through interpersonal confrontation, self-disclosure, and strong emotional expression."

140

All the students in the course — to one degree or another — are Duberman acolytes, believers in this charismatic, gifted teacher. Several students here tonight are close friends of mine, especially Jim. But there are many here whom I barely know; listening to this psychologist's expectations, I find it impossible to imagine revealing my deepest self to these people.

The leader, who looks to be about 40, reads the room, silent for a few moments as he shifts his gaze from one student to another. He then concludes his introduction with an emphatic imperative: "Here, we will face our inner selves."

I'm tempted to bolt immediately. I'm well acquainted with my inner self, and it's already way too talkative and loud; the last thing I want to do is turn up the volume, or give it a larger platform. But I resist the impulse to leave, out of loyalty to Martin and, honestly, bare curiosity — wanting to hear what others have to say, and to learn whether they're equally haunted by their "inner selves."

So I sit quietly, as far as I can get from the wooden chair in the center of the room. I'm listening. Nothing more.

The first person to speak is a woman — one of the few in my class of '71 — and she eloquently describes what it's like for her and her fellow females at Princeton.

"I feel like a Martian here," she says, looking around the roomful of men. A small woman dressed in a red sweater and jeans, her size and appearance make her conspicuous here, too. "It's so strange to be 'the only' everywhere. Our small classes always have only one, maybe two women. I'm rarely ever in a class with another woman. I've never had a woman professor.

"We can't join eating clubs because most of them aren't coed. So that doesn't make us feel too welcome. At the bars, some men are all over us like animals. Others say — under their breath — 'Girls, go home.'"

The psychologist speaks up. "How does that make you feel?"

141

"Very frustrated!" she says, with her arms crossed. " At Dillon Gym, there aren't even any basketballs for girls. No equipment. No women's athletics! Nothing!"

The psychologist grimaces. Obviously, he's looking for something more emotional than an equal-rights complaint.

"How can you help the men in the room understand your feelings? What are three emotional words you'd use to describe your experience? Are there other times when you've felt this way?"

His questions sound rehearsed and pat, even to my inexperienced ears. The student, now angry, snaps right back: "How would it make *you* feel?"

Things are tough enough for her as an outsider here, I'm thinking; she's not about to open herself up to ridicule or further isolation. The psychologist gives up and moves on.

The next student explains that he comes from a long line of family practice doctors who run an office in a small town in Connecticut. "The practice has been handed down from my great-grandfather to my grandfather to my father. And now they want me to become a doctor and take over. But I can't stand the sight of blood."

"How does this make you feel?" the psychologist asks again.

The cautious student shrugs his shoulders.

The psychologist talks briefly about parental expectations and asks the group how we think this student should handle this situation. Nobody says anything, so the psychologist offers his advice, encouraging the student to speak honestly and directly to his parents about his interests and career path.

Then he turns to face all of us. "I'm not sure you understand the purpose of this group," he says, with a hint of impatience. "This is not a political forum or a career counseling center. You are telling your stories, but we want you to go deeper emotionally. We want to learn what drives you and your reactions. You need to really get in touch with your feelings."

Even before he finishes, I'm slowly, steadily inching myself closer to the door. My curiosity has evaporated at the prospect of hearing such blatant displays of emotion.

I've almost reached the threshold when Martin booms my name.

"Bruce!"

Heads swivel; all eyes dart toward me, the human bull's-eye. Though I haven't said a word yet, I already feel exposed — and terrified. A violent shudder rattles my entire body.

Then Martin says the words I'm dreading: "Your turn."

Heart pounding, throat tightening, I'm a deer in headlights. I doubt I can speak, even if I wanted to.

"You've been sitting on the sidelines," Martin says calmly, in the soothing voice that's now so familiar to me. "What's holding you back?"

No answer.

"Come on now," Martin presses, gently but with determination. "I know you have a lot to contribute to this group."

Staring helplessly at Martin, I realize he's imploring me to demonstrate the great value of his daring experiment by taking center stage and sharing my deepest self.

Martin knows my pain — but he also knows that I would never want to disappoint him. I scan my friends: some sitting on the floor, others crowded together on the sofas, like a woven basket of support. Can I trust them?

I draw in a couple of deep breaths. My mind shouts NO as my body gets up off the floor and takes a few steps into the center of the room.

Looking around again nervously, I catch Jim's compassionate eyes. His warmth encourages me to jump into the icy waters of confession.

Clearing my throat, I take a seat on the wooden chair, in front of everyone. I scan the faces; all eyes are on me. It feels like I'm in a witness box, about to endure a brutal cross-examination. My knee begins bouncing uncontrollably, and I press one hand down hard on my leg to stop it.

"I... I don't know where to begin." I wipe my sweaty palms on my jeans. "I don't know all of you, and... well, I'm not sure what to say." I stop to breathe, knowing there's no escape.

"I guess I'll start by saying that I... I've never really felt like I... well, like I fit in here."

Even as I say these words, I think: *This is either shockingly brave or stupidly self-destructive, and I'll probably regret it later.* But I'm in the deep end now. Got to keep swimming.

"All... all of you seem so comfortable at Princeton." My eyes narrow as I scrutinize the faces that are studying mine. "Everyone here seems to have their shit together."

A few people guffaw, and their response gives me a little comfort. "Yeah, maybe not," I say, trying to smile but hearing the nerves in my wobbly voice.

I look at the psychologist, who approvingly nods his head up and down. Then I glance over at Martin, who is pumping his fist to encourage me to keep going.

"But... but I didn't go to a private school, like most of you. I don't come from money." I stop, swallow, then remind them of the gigantic power differential that sets me apart. "Some of you have seen me at my job in the dining room in Stevenson Hall. I'm the dishwasher."

No one reacts, so I go on

"I know all of us are dealing with the war. It just gets longer and longer. But not all of you are constantly worried about a terrible lottery number. I can hardly think about anything else. I am 90."

When I hear myself say 90 out loud, my head hurts; my heart races; beads of sweat form on my forehead. "That number," I say slowly, softly. "It terrifies me. Terrorizes me.

"Who knew a number could have so much power? I... I mean, it's just two digits on a piece of paper. A goddamn mathematical symbol — a stupid *numeral!* It's just supposed to be a way to count or measure something.

"But for me, 90 is everything. It's... it's like a living thing to me. 90 is behind whatever I say or do, every decision I make — getting serious with someone, whether to protest or demonstrate, if I can even go to law school.

"That fucking number is always chasing me. It's robbed me of my freedom! It makes me feel like I don't have a life of my own. Makes me question everything I think I know about myself."

Some classmates — maybe the ones who also have terrible lottery numbers — look at me tenderly. I take a deep breath and, basking in their empathy, stop speaking for a minute or so. Then, I go on.

"I know I can't... I just can't kill. Anyone. In a war, anywhere. I just can't." These are the private thoughts that loop constantly through my mind; now, I hear the words rushing out of my mouth. "But I don't know what to do about it. I don't feel like I could live with myself if I went to Canada to avoid the draft. Or got some doctor to write me a fake medical excuse.

"But also... I can't stand the thought of going to prison. Me? A convicted felon?" I shake my head, baffled by that thought.

"I've applied to be a CO, but I don't know if I'll get it. I don't even know if that's what I am, either." My voice is the only sound in the room. Martin is still nodding, urging me along. So is the psychologist. *Go deeper. Go deeper.*

"I don't have anyone to guide me," I say, identifying the core of my isolation. "My dad was in the service, but he's dead. He died five years ago, and I miss him every day. Especially now."

I drop my head and gulp for air. Then, hard as I've tried to swallow my emotions, the worst happens: tears roll down my face.

"Sometimes, I think, if he were here, he'd have all the answers. He could tell me what to do. But he's not here, and I have no idea what he'd say. Hard as I try — and I try all the time — I can barely hear his voice anymore."

Wiping my wet eyes on my flannel shirt sleeve, I notice the woman who spoke first staring at me piercingly. Tears are running down her cheeks, too. Even some of the guys on the couch look shaken.

"And my mother," I plow on, "well, she thinks all my life decisions are rash and reckless. All we do is fight. It's awful!" I pause to sniff, almost past caring what anyone thinks.

"You know, every night on the news, you see all those body bags coming home from Vietnam. I guess someone in Washington is counting the dead. But there are other casualties you can't see. Right here in America. The way the war is dividing families. *Destroying* families. I've got my own wounds with my mom. And —" now I'm sniffing — "after all this, I'm not sure I'll ever be able to have a decent relationship with her again."

I hear a few people grunt in agreement, revealing that they too have a fractured or ruined relationship with a mother or father.

"I just don't know what to do," I gasp. "And I feel so alone."

I drop my head into my hands and cover my eyes, trying to stop myself from completely breaking down. Then, I feel a hand on my shoulder, and I see that it's Martin's. I look up at him, and he gives me a gentle smile. Without my noticing, he and several of my friends have gathered around me. They touch my arms empathetically. Jim is standing next to me. Ringed by my classmates, I can feel my shame and fear melt away. Tears now flowing freely, I lean into the circle of acceptance and support. Some in the group — people I don't even know — touch my shoulder or even bend down to hug me.

I feel as if I've finally set down the heavy weight I've been carrying. Or maybe I've torn off the mask I've been wearing for all of my Princeton years. I've twisted, turned, pretzeled myself trying to fit in here; now, for the first time, I've shown my classmates who I really am. And, miraculously, in this moment I feel safe and accepted.

"I feel strange," I say, looking up at the psychologist, "... strangely released."

He grins at me. "*That's* what I'm talking about."

Though our three-hour marathon is far from over, I'm spent: completely out of the energy required to focus any longer, let alone process what has happened to me tonight. I return to my spot near the door and quietly wait for the encounter session to end.

Then, I walk downstairs into the night, feeling lighter and heavier at the same time. The dark, refreshing autumn air helps clear my mind. I head toward my dorm room. Blissfully alone.

But the bliss can't last.

In the morning, as usual, I meet Ric for breakfast. The moment I see the smirk on his face, I know something's up.

As we order our eggs and toast, I narrow my eyes and ask him point-blank. "What's happening, Sheldon? Come on, let me in on the joke!"

He doesn't answer. Instead, as he takes his breakfast plate from the cook, he looks over at me, raises his eyebrows, and blurts out a quick, mocking laugh.

A stone drops from my throat to my heart. In his taunt, Ric has instantly conveyed the reaction I feared.

I should have known! In a place this small — this small-minded — rumors of the slightest deviation from "normal" behavior spread like a California wildfire.

"Hey, Jerome!" Ric sniggers, as we take our seats across from each other at the table. I recall the kind, compassionate faces of the students in last night's encounter group; suddenly, their expressions morph from sensitivity to sneers.

I brace myself as Ric reaches into his sweatshirt pocket, pulls out a crumpled ball of Kleenex, and tosses it at me.

Ducking, I dodge the Kleenex as Ric sinks his shot. "Jerome! Still in touch with your *feelings?*"

DECEMBER 1970

For as long as I could remember, I had believed my destiny would be linked with the African-American struggle for inclusion, equality, and justice. My father may have planted this idea through his great admiration for the Boston Celtics' Bill Russell, who was not just a basketball star, but a strong, uncompromising Black man and an agent for political change.

Just after our family moved to San Diego in 1963, controversy erupted at my new junior high school when administrators hired the first Black teacher. Some parents requested white teachers for their children; mine insisted that I be assigned to Harold K. Brown's physical education class.

Coach Brown, a dignified community activist known universally as Hal, was helping to desegregate not only my school, but also San Diego's housing. Occasionally, I would visit his small office after school to ask him about the racial divide in my new city and how he was addressing the problems. These powerful, intimate conversations inspired me and planted the seeds of my quiet resistance.

Throughout my adolescence, I was consumed by the moral power of the civil rights movement. As the struggle for racial equality intensified, I admired the courage of non-violent activists, like Dr. King, as they attempted to bend the arc of history.

After King's assassination in 1968, dozens of colleges and universities, including Princeton, began to recognize the need to create academic spaces devoted to Black history, literature, and culture. A Princeton report on the subject called for establishing a program dedicated to researching and teaching African-American culture — and more. "Though the program will be open to all students," the report stated, "one of its advantages will be to make this campus more hospitable for the Black students who are arriving in increasing numbers."

Thus began a program that developed into a distinguished example of what the discipline could be. By the 1980s, Princeton was attracting such scholarly stars as the celebrated author Toni Morrison, the historian and political activist Cornel West, and the American historian and visual artist Nell Painter. Their prestige helped place the Department of African American studies among the top programs of its kind nationwide. Professors Morrison and Painter also were Princeton's first female African-American faculty members.

I'm honored to serve on the committee charged with making the program a reality. Personally, I believe the Afro-American studies program can help me understand the Black experience and prepare me for the next steps in my life's journey. So it is with excitement and anticipation that, in the fall of 1970, I enroll as one of the program's initial twenty-eight students.

To announce its existence, Princeton decides to send a representative to a Black Studies conference in Atlanta that will bring together students in similar programs from campuses around the country. This haphazard decision finds nobody eager to leave campus in December, just before winter break. I'm the only one to jump at this opportunity to see what life is like on a Black campus in Atlanta, home to some of the top historically Black colleges and universities: Clark, Spelman, Morris Brown, Morehouse.

Of course, I realize that not many white students are likely to attend the conference. I could very well find myself as the only white guy in a room of Blacks, most of them wondering what the hell I'm doing there. But I figure I need to push myself, trusting that the experience will be broadening and worth my time.

And I have another reason to go. This is a chance to see my Atlanta relatives: my dad's sister, Aunt Eileen; her husband, Uncle Alex, and my cousins Stanley, Jerry, and Donnie. The last time I visited them was during the summer of 1965, when I was still reeling from Dad's recent death.

That summer, Alex did his best to fill in for my father. I understood this and loved him for it. Knowing how I worshiped Sandy Koufax, the storied left-handed pitcher for the Los Angeles Dodgers, Alex invited me to join his family in attending the Dodgers' entire three-game series against the Atlanta Braves. In those sweltering Georgia evenings, I was thrilled to witness the Dodgers' three best pitchers — Don Drysdale, Claude Osteen, and Koufax — face an incredible Braves line-up that included the stellar third baseman Eddie Matthews and the incomparable right fielder, "Hammerin' Hank" Aaron.

"Hey, Bruce!" Alex greets me heartily as I step through the door and into the familiar living room, which hasn't changed a bit in five years. My uncle and I hug heartily, pounding each other's backs. Then, he holds me at arm's length, grasping my shoulders to look me up and down. I see myself through his eyes – I'm four inches taller, and I've got a lot more facial hair compared to my last visit, when Alex carefully taught me how to shave the peach fuzz on my upper lip.

"Not a boy anymore," Alex smiles, summarizing my appearance. "You look good, son." He gestures me into a comfortable chair as he takes his own place on the luxurious brown leather La-Z-Boy recliner. "Now, what brings you here?"

151

"Thanks," I grin, warm and happy in his approval. "I'm here for a conference at Morehouse for students in the new African-American studies programs around the country." The moment I speak these words, my stomach begins to churn as I remember Alex's casual, life-long racism.

"Oh! And you're going to take MARTA to the 'schvartze' college?" That vulgar word immediately causes my teeth to clench; the hairs on my neck stand up like the fur of an angry dog.

During my visits to their home, Alex never used the ubiquitous, pejorative "N word;" he substituted *schvartze* — a derogatory Yiddish term rooted in the German word *schvarts,* meaning black. He talked about "those people" — including "the good ones," whom he praised as loyal employees at work — but "the good ones" were few and far between. More typical were "the other ones," whom he ridiculed for qualities he considered more representative of the entire race.

"Well, yeah, Uncle Alex," Trying to be polite, I bristle nonetheless. I hadn't thought about it until this minute, but now I'm struck by how uncomfortable it'll be to stay in Alex's house while attending a Black Studies conference.

How can I be around these people I need and love and, at the same time, engage in this talk that makes me sick? Do I swallow my anger and disappointment? Should I speak up, insulting their hospitality? I feel that all the good I'm doing in creating Princeton's program is colliding with the deeply rooted racism in my own family.

"You do know what MARTA means, don't you?"

I look at him quizzically. Of course I know that MARTA is the Metropolitan Atlanta Rapid Transit Authority. Alex cocks his head playfully, as he does when telling a joke or feeling the need to dominate a conversation.

"It means 'Moving *Africans* Rapidly Through Atlanta.'" Alex chokes with laughter at his witticism. But, when he sees my face redden with rage, his body stiffens.

Alex is a handsome, muscular man; according to my mother, who remarks often on the resemblance, he looks a lot like Paul Newman, one of Hollywood's great heartthrobs of the 1960s. Like Newman, Alex has piercing blue eyes and curly brown hair. Entirely apart from Newman, Alex is justifiably proud of the life he has made for himself and his family: his devoted wife Eileen (whom he always calls 'Leen), their three accomplished sons, and 'Leen's mother, my grandmother Alice, who has lived with the family since Alex returned from the Pacific theater after World War II.

"C'mon now, Bruce." He gestures with his hands to calm down. "I didn't mean anything by it."

Jabbing his index finger toward my chest, he offers a recommendation. "You've got to learn to loosen up and laugh a little bit, son. Don't take everything so seriously. Hell, the *schvartzes* have never had it so good. The government does everything for them now."

Words catch in my throat. "Uncle Alex," I finally spit out, "I... I just don't find anything funny about it."

"Never mind, boy," he interrupts, pressing on. "Now, 'Leen tells me you're one of those draft-card burners. That so?"

I'd like to slink out of this beautiful northern Atlanta split-level home and run miles away. Or maybe just crawl under a rock. Anything to distance myself from Alex. How did this conversation go off the rails so fast?

"Uncle Alex," I begin, trying to be more direct and honest, hoping to defuse the tensions and questions that are certain to arise while I'm here. "I... I know you're a vet. So was my dad. I can't imagine the guts it took for you to fight overseas. But I... I'm not like you... or my dad."

Alex's blue eyes blaze as his face turns crimson, but I keep going. "I'm not going to fight in this war... or any war."

I look hard at my only uncle, and I flash on my Dad's blue eyes. Dad and Alex were brothers-in-law, but complete opposites about race issues. Though they grew up in the same culture, with the same prejudices, Dad had left the South for Seattle as a young man. In time, through his broader experiences, he confronted and was deeply disturbed by America's injustices; repudiating the racial bigotry of his upbringing, he committed himself to equality.

When it comes to the war, though, both men may have held the same views. This is probably the conversation I would have had with Dad about my decision to become a CO.

"Am I scared of what's going to happen to me?" I keep going. "Damn right I am. But I have to do what my conscience says is right. No disrespect to you, and no disrespect to America."

Without a word, Alex rises abruptly from his La-Z-Boy, swiftly crosses the room in long strides, and steps out into the crisp winter air on the deck. I watch him through the window, his back to me, gazing off into the distance. I can't move. Fixed in my chair, I'm hoping Aunt Eileen will sense the sudden silence as her cue to swoop in and save me.

* * *

The next day, Aunt Eileen invites me to go out to lunch. I have a visceral love for 'Leen, whose fair skin and wide-set eyes so resemble Dad's. At 50, she's still sweet and pleasant-looking. Having lived her entire life in the South, she speaks with a distinctive drawl, extending my name into two syllables, "Be-ruuce" — a unique and endearing pronunciation. 'Leen avoids controversial topics, preferring to steer conversations to her beloved Braves or Georgia Tech's Ramblin' Wreck football team.

Eileen takes me to a new fast-food restaurant called Chick-fil-A. My aunt has a story for every occasion, and today is no different. As we stand in line, waiting to place our order, she explains how she's acquainted with Mr. S. Truett Cathy, the man who started this small chain. Mr. Cathy attended Boys High when my father was a four-sports star at Marist, a smaller school in the same conference. Since Eileen closely followed my dad's teams, she knew all the local high-school athletes at that time.

Unlike the Varsity, Atlanta's most famous drive-in, Chick-fil-A offers only a modest menu, from which Eileen orders their specialty: chicken sandwiches, one for each of us. Remembering that I love onion rings and fries, she orders extras of both.

We take a seat by the window. 'Leen carefully unwraps her sandwich and then rewraps it, just as carefully, so she can take a few bites without getting her hands messy. She eats slowly, occasionally gazing out the window. I can tell 'Leen has something on her mind. I enthusiastically chomp on my food, not saying much, expecting she'll talk when she's ready.

"Be-ruuuce," she says finally, putting down her half-eaten sandwich. "Don't pay Alex no mind." She waves her hand dismissively, as if swatting at a bothersome fly. "He's always spouting off about one thing or another."

"He does it to me, too," she drawls softly. "In fact, when we're with other couples, he's always teasin' me, sayin' things like, 'If you want to know my opinion on something, just ask 'Leen.' I only *wish* he'd listen to me and take on some of my opinions! Instead, all of us have to put up with his outrageous ideas."

Last night, during dinner, I'd remembered how 'Leen and the family have always dealt with Alex and his obnoxious tirades. When he goes off, they gently razz him, firing back with "Is that a fact, Alex?" or "Where on earth did you come up with that, Dad?" I'm used to the tense, quiet meals in my mother's house; here, family dinners are

155

raucous affairs, with lively banter, rapid passing of plates, and all sorts of kibitzing — mostly about what they're about to eat. "I could get better food than this at the Varsity," someone will toss out provocatively. Then one of the boys will pipe up, "Better service, too."

'Leen daintily takes another bite out of her sandwich. "You're my brother's only son, and, you know, I often tell Alex, you're not that different from him."

"Really?" My eyebrows shoot up. I don't look anything like Dad; in fact, I've often thought about how much I'm *not* like him. He seemed to have it all — good looks, athletic gifts, an easy charm, lots of friends. I stare at 'Leen, hoping she'll elaborate.

"You know, Be-ruuuce," she goes on, "Joe and I had it tough as kids. Our father died young, too. Grandma Alice didn't have any skills, and even if she did, there weren't any jobs. The Depression hit us hard. We didn't have any money, so Joe did whatever he could — mowing lawns, delivering newspapers and groceries, working as a soda jerk — to keep us from going hungry."

"But, 'Leen..." I try to interrupt her. I've heard all this before; now I want her to explain how Dad and I are alike.

"Sports saved your father." She ignores me, strolling toward her point. "He never was a reader, never liked school all that much. He was a practical joker, always loved making people laugh." She looks out again with a small smile; she's probably lost in some memory of one of Joe's long-ago pranks.

"Aunt Eileen," I say, startling her. "Please! Tell me how I'm like my father?"

"Now, you stop interrupting me," she drawls, "and eat your ... your..." Eileen holds up a deep-fried tidbit, puzzling over it. "What do you call these, anyway? Fries, I guess." The "fry" has a weird shape; it looks like a miniature waffle.

"Eat those things before they get cold," she commands, dipping one into the pool of catsup on a napkin. Instead of taking a bite, she looks at it suspiciously and sets it aside.

"What I'm trying to say is, in big ways — the most important ways — you are very much your father's son. If your father gave his word, you could depend on him. He took responsibility seriously. Never cut corners, always so me-*tic*-u-lous. He used humor to hide his worries from Mother and me, but I could see him fret."

She stops, looks down at my hands, and blurts, "He bit his nails something awful." My face flushes with embarrassment, and I quickly tuck one of my hands under my thigh.

"Now, Be-ruuuce, I don't pretend to know anything about this here Vietnam." Her drawl thickens as she measures each word. "I'm glad my boys are in school, away from all the goings-on.

"But... your mother has written to me about you. She's very worried about what you're doing. She thinks she's going to lose you... to the war, or to God knows what causes you're involved in."

She stops, dabs another peculiar waffle-fry in some catsup, examines it again, and takes a tiny, tentative bite of the corner.

"I can tell you this, and now I'm speaking as your father's older sister. I knew Joe better than anyone; I watched him grow up. And believe you me, we were heartbroken when he left for Seattle – even though we knew he was happy with his new family.

"Whenever he called me on the phone, he couldn't stop bragging about his only son. 'Such a fine ballplayer! Such a great student! Such a sensitive, caring, conscientious boy!'"

I sit quietly, my lunch forgotten. I guess I'm hoping that she can provide what I've yearned for since I was 15. Someone to bring my father back to me... someone who could give me his benediction.

"Most of all, he talked about your character. He *valued* who you are and how much you worried about current events. How upset you were about President Kennedy's assassination. How angry you were at those folks — yes, like us — who had prejudice against Negroes."

"But you know, honey." Her voice drops to a whisper. "Joe, like Alex, was a veteran. He proudly spent his life working for the government. He believed deeply in America and all that it's given our family, and he always went on about how we owe our country our loyalty."

My shoulders slump. I thought Aunt Eileen was the one person I could count on to understand me, maybe even take my side. Instead, I'm afraid she's going to pick up where Professor Garvey, Coach Eiler, and Mom left off.

"Honestly, I think your father would be very upset with your decision about this war," she chides. "This is not his way."

I drop my head, bracing myself to be chastised again. This one's going to really hurt.

"But, Be-ruuuce." I look up and see that she's holding up a cautionary finger.

"He's your father, first, last, and always. He'd listen to you, even if that meant hearing things he didn't want to hear. He'd try to understand how you see the world, even if it goes against everything he stands for. And I *know* — no matter what — he'd never stop loving you. Never."

I pick up the paper napkin in my lap and dab at my tears. Aunt Eileen, seeing my deep emotions, tries to push me toward compassion. "Don't be too hard on your mother. She's worried sick about you and she doesn't have Joe to support her anymore. In her own way, she's telling you she loves you."

'Leen reaches over the table and takes my hand to underscore what she's just said. I release a big sigh.

"And about Uncle Alex..." I look at her skeptically. Does she intend to address the blunders of *every* family member?

"I hope you can ignore what he said last night. He runs off at the mouth, not thinking about how he's hurting someone. He does that to the boys all the time, and I always have to bail him out of the mess. It's not easy.

"But what you heard last night — well, he probably wasn't just talking to you. He's worried about our sons, too, but he doesn't know what to say to them... so he said it to you."

"'Leen." Looking up, I face her directly. "I'm scared and worried and upset, all the time. It means a lot to me to just talk. And have you listen to me." I let that sink in... for both of us.

"You know, this is one of the first decisions I'll make for myself... as a man. I've made up my mind, and I'm at peace."

Now, tears glisten her eyes. "And that's what your dad would want for you," she says softly. "To be your own man." She looks away and blinks, trying to hide her own raw emotions.

Turning back to me, she releases my hand, picks up a now-droopy fry, and narrows her eyes at it. "And who in God's name came up with this waffle thing anyway? S. Truett Cathy?"

Determined to lighten the conversation, she grins. "I'm not sure whether to dip it in catsup or douse it in maple syrup!"

* * *

Where should I sit?

Here at Morehouse to observe a class in African-American history, I'm standing at the door of the large, horseshoe-shaped classroom, searching for an empty seat. The lecture has already started, and I recognize the material from the survey I took last year — one of the first courses in Princeton's new program.

"Last week, we talked about the horrors of post-Reconstruction life here in the South." The African-American professor, trim in a charcoal gray three-piece suit, stands behind a lectern sitting atop a table. He speaks precisely in a strong voice.

"By the turn of the 20th century, there emerged two voices offering solutions to the perpetual problem of American racism. They were very different approaches: one was protest; the other was accommodation..."

Finally spotting an open seat, I step into the classroom. Instantly, thirty heads swivel in my direction. Sixty eyes blister my face. Even the professor suspends his lecture. The room falls into ominous silence.

I'm not just late. I am the only white.

My presence provokes a palpable hostility in the classroom. But what have I done?

I notice that some of the men are wearing dashikis — those loose-fitting tunics whose bright colors and intricate patterns proudly declare a West African heritage. I look like a stupid-ass white boy in my gray Princeton sweatshirt and flared corduroys.

Still trying not to call attention to myself, I slip into a seat near the door and unpack my notebook and pens. The lecturer is comparing W. E. B. DuBois with Booker T. Washington, contrasting their respective models of responding to racism.

Instead of taking notes, I start writing down questions about my choice to study in a program designed specifically for African-Americans.

Is there a place for people like me in programs like this?

If I participate in any discussion — and I probably won't — will Black students assume that I speak for *all* whites?

Is this what a Black kid feels like when he is the only African-American in a class of whites?

In this room, I feel I have no voice. I want to defend my purpose and my right to be here, but I doubt anyone wants to hear from me. Yet I fear that if I say nothing, my silence will be perceived as cowardice or indifference.

As the lecturer continues, I think about how much I respected DuBois when I read his writings last year. I appreciated his insistence on complete political and social equality.

Yet, here, I'm definitely unequal — and definitely unwelcome. Students occasionally glare at me with anger, resentment, and disgust. These Morehouse students clearly don't want me in their territory.

Given that our destinies are intertwined, I've always believed in the possibilities of interracial friendship. Now, I'm "the other," with no chance of integrating into a larger whole.

Times have changed; the defiant principles of Black Pride and Black Power have replaced the hopeful chorus of "We Shall Overcome." Seems like I'm about five years too late — pathetically optimistic, frozen in a more auspicious time when whites and Blacks, Jews and gentiles could work together for a better America.

As the professor delivers his final remarks, I quickly duck out of the lecture hall. Breathing a sigh of relief, I walk through beautiful old Graves Hall and recall a searing passage from Ralph Ellison's "Invisible Man."

"I am a man of substance, of flesh and bone, fiber and liquids — and I might even be said to possess a mind. I am invisible, understand, simply because people refuse to see me."

At Morehouse — humbled, humiliated, denigrated and despised, just because of my skin color — I am the invisible man.

Spring Semester

The calendar flips to 1971, and suddenly, I have only five months till graduation. I spend much of January working on my thesis, taking regular breaks to play basketball at Dillon Gym, and loading up on kitchen shifts at Stevenson.

On a cold Friday night, I join a small group of sports fans in Jadwin Gym to watch Princeton's basketball team take on Harvard. With radical politics still dominating campus life, enthusiasm for sports has diminished drastically; it's always easy to find good seats when only political conservatives and sports junkies, like me, show up for home games.

I'm proud of the fact that, except for my bout with meningitis, I've attended every one of Princeton's football games — even though the team has fallen off its usual perch at the top of the Ivy League. During my first two years at Princeton, I went to all the basketball games as well, and I saw some phenomenally gifted players. This year, however, the team isn't as strong, and fewer people are coming to the games. On this particular night, Jadwin is not crowded.

Midway through the first half, Harvard brings in a substitute whose long, dark hair is secured by a headband. Behind me, some nasty Princeton fans immediately begin to whoop "Indian war cries."

"Woo-woo-woo-woo! *Woo*-woo-woo-woo!" Slapping his hand across his mouth, one idiotic fan starts the chant, which spreads and echoes, all around the gym, louder and louder, uglier and uglier.

Everywhere I go, racism seems to bubble beneath every surface. Here, again, Princeton students are mocking Indigenous people, just as they did during that speech last spring. It was stupid and offensive then; it's stupid and offensive now. Why is this group targeted so often, so viciously?

Rage floods me. Fists tight, I jump up, turn around, and glare at the mob, all outfitted in Princeton's proud orange and black.

"Shut the fuck *up!*"

Instantly, it's *me* they're taunting, dumping their *"woo*-woo-woo-woo" on me, regurgitating all the shit Hollywood has fed them in "cowboy and Indian" movies.

Worse, the band now picks up their chant, the bass drum vigorously thumping a noisy tom-tom beat. *"BOOM-boom-boom-boom. BOOM-boom-boom-boom."*

The insistent throbbing, the hollering all around me — it's not just infuriating, it's frightening. This angry mob is targeting *me.*

I'm enraged — and now I'm scared, too. Grabbing my paperback book, I push past the yelling, jeering crowd, out into the cold night. The lopsided score in Princeton's favor leaves little doubt as to the outcome of the game. Not that I care anymore.

When I get to my room, still burning mad, I dash off an angry letter to the editor at the *Daily Princetonian.* I know the typewritten statement sounds bombastic and self-righteous, but I don't care. Instead of editing, I run the letter over to the newspaper office immediately, to meet the deadline for Friday's edition.

The letter appears on January 22, 1971, under the headline: "'Degrading' war-whoops and tom-tom beats." It read, in part:

We watch the Indian lose in Westerns on television; now we beat the Indian in the cozy confines of Jadwin Gymnasium...

When the crowd elects to deride a member of its own race with the symbols of a despised race, it rips at the fabric of what we claim to be — a civilized society... it is not enough that Princeton does not give one goddamn about the Indian's condition — that the Indian has a life expectancy of twenty years less as contrasted to any other minority group, that the most frequent cause of death among adolescent Indians is suicide. Rather it is more convenient, and fun, to mock them and degrade whatever symbols of identity and meaning the whites have allowed the Indian to keep.

Perhaps all this concern over an innocent bit of fun is uncalled for. But then, if there are never any Indians in our lives, and we are unconcerned and complicit in the repudiation of their existences, what would one expect of a Princeton crowd? And, anyway, we won the game.

The letter stirs up hostility all day, everywhere I go.

At breakfast, Ric curls his lips in a sardonic smile when he asks: "You going native on me, Jerome? You gonna help out at Alcatraz?" He's talking about the 19-month-long protest by Native Americans and their supporters who are occupying Alcatraz Island, demonstrating against past wrongs and current discrimination.

"Why are there so many assholes on this campus, Ric?" I snap back, raising my eyebrows to let him know that, right now, I think he's one of them.

"What's with you, Jerome?" he says. "Just ignore all the shit that flies."

But it's getting harder and harder to look away. On my way to Stevenson to work a lunch shift, I have to walk past the clubs I despise on Prospect Avenue. By now most upperclassmen know each other; with my letter having trumpeted my position, everyone in the clubs knows me.

When I approach Cannon Club, several members are standing out front, next to its huge eponymous weapon mounted on its front walkway. When they see me, they erupt in another chorus of "Indian war cries." I flip them the bird and keep on walking.

Down the street, I pass Cottage and Ivy, the two most restrictive clubs, whose members brag that their endowments are greater than the entirety of Brown University's. At both clubs, several guys come up and bombard me with questions. "What's wrong with you, Bruce?" "Why are you always so angry?" "Why can't you take a joke?"

Things get worse later at Stevenson, where I'm cornered by one of the professors who often joins students for a meal. This professor is known as kind and caring; students respect him and often seek his counsel.

"Bruce, you need to stop taking things so seriously." Puffing gravely on his meerschaum pipe, his cloud of smoke enveloping us, he keeps his voice down as he lectures me, careful not to involve others in this private repudiation.

"Those boys didn't mean anything, Bruce. It was just for laughs."

He's in their camp, too. I shake my head in disbelief.

"Besides," he continues, "I'm sure that wasn't the first time that player heard war whoops. And..." the professor waves a hand dismissively, "if he doesn't want to be the butt of jokes, all he needs to do is cut his hair."

"Racism is racism, Professor," I snap. "No matter how you dress it up. What am I supposed to do, sit there and laugh with them? Join them? Maybe paint my face red and act like Tonto?"— the Native American sidekick to the Lone Ranger on the popular television series of the past decade.

"Hold on, Bruce," he snaps right back, "I'm not here to get into a discussion of American history. All I'm trying to do is to protect you from yourself. You keep acting like this and, I'm telling you, you're going to find yourself alienated from the entire community."

The next few weeks show me that he's right. Jim writes me a reassuring note, encouraging me to continue the fight. Other friends simply disappear — as if they're quarantining themselves from some contagious disease I carry.

A few months before graduation, I realize that I had only one Black professor in all my four years. I'm bothered by the diaphanous veil of racism that hangs over Princeton.

When I talk to Jim about it, he tells me about the prestigious writing seminar he's taking. Led by the author Anthony Burgess, whose work includes the notorious "A Clockwork Orange," the seminar meets at Ivy, the most elite of Princeton's eating clubs. In this elevated atmosphere, Jim tells me, drinks are served by silent African-American waiters wearing formal, starched white tunics. To summon a servant, someone at the seminar table rings a bell — as if the whole scene were taking place on a plantation in the antebellum South.

As my final semester starts in February, Cleve beckons me to join him at the table in the back of Stevenson's kitchen. As is his custom whenever he wants to talk about something serious, he entices me with dinner: tonight, a heaping plate of roast beef, mashed potatoes, and green beans.

I dive into the delicious meal so hungrily that I hardly notice Cleve hasn't said a word. When I finally look up, I see that he's looking intently at me.

"Listen, Hondo!" Cleve always calls me "Hondo," the nickname for the Celtics' player John Havlicek, because he believes my long side-burns resemble Havlicek's looks.

"When you goin' get off your skimpy white ass and start involving us in this place?" Last fall, Cleve had chided me several times about Stevenson's near "lily-whiteness." Why is he bringing this up again?

Confused and angry, I glare at him, wondering what he expects of me.

He massages his forehead with his fingers, then narrows his eyes at me. "Hondo. What good is Community House if the kids can't come here to see what life is like?"

Community House is an after-school program where several under-graduates, including me, have mentored local Black kids for the past year. I've often thought about how these kids live so close, yet so far away from the Princeton universe. And I've wondered how I could make the place more real for them.

"How you think they feel, never being invited to your home?" Cleve asks. "You think you too good for us?" He knows how to bait me.

"So what are you saying, Cleve? That we should have them come up for a meal every week?"

"That's right, Hondo. Maybe on Friday nights."

"I don't know, Cleve." I've stopped eating; he has my attention. "Caddy runs a tight ship here. I mean... I'm willing, but you know, things could go wrong, and Caddy —"

"I got Caddy," he says. "We gotta do *somethin'* to make this place less honky." Cleve stands up, looks down at me and says, "Don't y'think I'd like to cook for some of my own?"

A few weeks later, we host our first Community House Friday night dinner for local African American youth, and Cleve prepares his finest down-home soul food: fried chicken, candied sweet potatoes, black-eyed peas, collard greens, cornbread. At first, the dinners are awkward. After all, Princeton students are four or five years older than the kids, most of whom are high-school juniors and seniors. Beyond the age gap, the well-intentioned but maladroit Stevensonians often stumble and blunder around the Black kids.

But we keep meeting, and by the time spring rolls around, everyone looks forward to the weekly event. The students and locals bond, thriving on teasing and laughter. Occasionally, Cleve comes into the dining room and proudly observes the boisterous event he initiated.

One Friday night late March, I take a seat next to Tyrone, a quiet high-school sophomore. Tyrone is short, bespectacled, with close-cropped hair; he generally sits at the far end of a table. Some Friday nights, when I don't have a dishwashing shift, we talk and, after dinner, go upstairs and listen to music together.

This night, Tyrone's attitude is different: less withdrawn, more hostile. "I like your food well enough, white boy," he sneers, "but don't think for a second I want to be like you."

His attitude and words are cutting. I never expected him to be like me, but I'm insulted that he calls me "white boy." I'm white, yes — but I'm not any old white boy.

"Tyrone, what's this about?" I ask, trying to keep the edge out of my voice.

"Look, Bruce, alla you sit 'round here, feel like you doin' something, but it don't mean shit," he growls. "Brothers dyin' over there, 'n' alla you keep your white asses clean. You read the *papers,* man? We gettin' killed over there... and for what? So I can sit and eat soul food with you every Friday night?"

"Tyrone!" Blood drains from my face; suddenly I'm queasy, and I don't know what to say. He's right, and we both know it.

"I hate this war as much as you, Tyrone. Maybe even more," I say slowly, not sure what to say. "I can't defend it. It's racist, it's terrible. And I don't know how to change things."

We stop talking, staring hard at each other across the racial divide. To Tyrone, I am both the cause and embodiment of his anger. As much as *I* despise being a Princetonian, to Tyrone that's exactly what I am: Princeton's privileged.

He smirks a little, then says playfully, "Look, man, I just messin' with you."

"Really?" I'm baffled and abashed. "'Cause I feel pretty shitty right now."

"Yeah, man. Sometimes things just come out. I just say stuff I'm thinkin'."

"But I'm thinking some of the same things," I say, "and, well... it really bothers me."

"We still good?" he asks.

I nod, relieved.

Tyrone jumps out of his chair and asks, "Wanna go upstairs and listen to music? Got any James Brown?"

But throughout the night, I keep thinking about what Tyrone said. I'm ashamed to have a student deferment while "the brothers" serve in my place. I keep hearing him: "Brothers dyin' over there, 'n' alla you keep your white asses clean."

And that thought, Tyrone, won't stop messing with me.

Spring 1971

In mid-April, just two months before graduation, spring erupts at Princeton. Entombed in my subterranean carrel at Firestone Library, where I'm finishing my senior thesis on Robert Kennedy's relationship with Black America, I've completely missed the verdant green of early buds and blooms.

Now, walking the campus, I find myself in quiet awe, struck once again by the beauty around me. Elm trees are leafing, perennials are flowering, and a single, huge gingko tree near the McCosh Walk is spreading its canopy of pale-green leaves. The famous maple tree, right outside of Witherspoon, reddens as it rouses back to life. A particularly serene elm tree near Prospect House draws me out of Firestone, providing a daily sense of calm and change.

When the Nassau Hall bell tolls at the top of each hour, I hear a new poignancy in its solemn peal. For more than 100 years, stealing the bell's clapper has been a popular stunt — but it's one prank I would never pull. I don't want to stop time.

Lately, I even find myself a little optimistic about my CO claim. A recent Supreme Court decision (*Welsh v. United States*), in clarifying what the court meant by the *Seeger* reference to comparable religious beliefs, actually broadens the eligibility for CO status. This development could cause the San Diego Draft Board to regard my application more favorably.

But I still haven't asked anyone for letters — even though Mary Ann Blaum's voice rings in my head, loud and clear, urging me to do just that.

"You've done all you can, Bruce, but your file lacks support," she said back in December, when I last saw her. At that time, my hair was longer than ever, curling down over my collar, while Mary Ann's was cut short, Twiggy-style. "Without the validation of others, your claim looks weak. Get me letters. They need to show the depth of your beliefs."

I did create a list in one of my notebooks of those I'll ask, but I'm stuck — too nervous to make the request. At the top of the page are Jim, Martin Duberman, and Professor Garvey. Jim and Martin are fierce critics of the war, and Garvey has expressed reservations, so I'm confident that they'll come through.

Next is Coach Eiler: I don't know whether he'll write from his hawkish perspective or from his personal understanding of my character. I've underlined his name several times. My entire claim might rest on Eiler.

One day in mid-April, I open the door of my dorm room and nearly trip over a surprise: a pile-up of mail containing not just greeting cards for my 22nd birthday, but also several fat envelopes, all shoved through the mail slot and landing in a jumble. I carefully step over the accumulation, stoop to collect them, and spread out all the mail on my bed.

Before ripping into the larger envelopes, I look out my window at the "New Quad" and watch students happily flipping a Frisbee back and forth. I think back to April of 1967, when I sat before another set of thick envelopes in my bedroom back in San Diego. Then, Princeton seemed like an unattainable dream.

In truth, I was numb for most of my teenage years, burying my sorrow beneath frantic activities and intense study at Clairemont High

School. Even though I graduated first in my class, many of my classmates were smarter, more intellectually inquisitive, more creative than I was. I stumbled through calculus, relying on constant assistance from my friends, and didn't even qualify for Honors English.

I really don't know why Princeton (and several other universities) accepted me. Straight-A students were a dime a dozen; practically everyone at Princeton had been a school or class president, a yearbook or newspaper editor, a star athlete. My SAT scores were in the bottom quartile of incoming freshmen; I stank as an athlete; I had no rich relatives, and I knew no one at the university. The only explanation I could think of is that one of my letters of recommendation — maybe Eiler's — was persuasive.

Now, I carefully slit open the envelopes and scan acceptances, along with offers of financial aid, from Boalt Hall, University of California (Berkeley); Santa Clara Law School, and my first choice, Stanford.

Hands shaking, I skim Stanford's letter quickly to glimpse my future:

> Dear Mr. Wasser:
>
> I take great pleasure in offering you admission to Stanford University's Law School Class of 1974. Congratulations! We know that you will bring something original and extraordinary to the intellectual life of our campus and look forward to having you join the Stanford community...

My heart pounds with elation... and fear. It's thrilling that I've accomplished this long-standing goal — but what if 90 robs me of this opportunity? Nixon has done nothing to de-escalate this endless war. The once vibrant anti-war movement has lost steam, and 90 is sure to be called soon. A student deferment is no longer an option: law students don't qualify, and my conscience wouldn't allow me to apply for one anyway.

The good news from Stanford creates a whole new set of worries. Will Stanford understand what being a CO means? Will they defer my admission if I have to perform alternative service? What if I go to jail? Would the law school even consider a convicted felon?

I swat away these dispiriting thoughts, shifting to the happy decision of whom to call first about my exciting news. There's really no question of who should get that honor: the one family member who has unconditionally loved me throughout my life, Grandma Rose.

Rose cherishes education, insisting that the American Dream depends upon learning. She sacrificed, scrimped, and saved so my mother could attend the University of Washington. Herself deprived of higher education, Rose often bragged about her certificate for outstanding achievement in handwriting. In fact, my own meticulous "hand" was inspired by Rose's pride in the Palmer Method of handwriting. Now, her only grandson is on track to become a lawyer!

Despite the expense of a daytime long-distance phone call, I dial her number. "Grandma Rose," I blurt out. "I heard from the law schools today. Stanford accepted me. I'm going to Stanford!"

"My *schoene hertzel*," Grandma Rose exclaims, "I'm so proud of you! I always knew you could do it. You'll be a fine attorney!"

Hoping to avoid running up the phone bill, I quickly share the details: when school starts, the generous financial aid package I received, whether I'll need to work during my studies. In this conversation, law school is a sure thing; I don't want to spoil this celebratory call by mentioning the cloud of 90.

"We should hang up," she says after a few minutes, concerned about the cost of the call. "Have you told your mother yet?"

"No..." I bite my lip. She knows how things are with my mother. "Not yet, Grandma."

"Brucie," Grandma Rose gently scolds me, "you need to call her right away. I know it's expensive, but I'll send you money. Call your mother. She loves you, and she'll be so proud to hear this news."

"OK, Grandma, OK," I say. "I love you, you know."

"I know, boychik, I know. And you know I love you, too! Now, call your mother."

I stare at my rotary phone, but I can't bring myself to dial Mom. I'll do it later, I tell myself. Instead, I roll a sheet of paper into my type-writer and click, "Dear Mr. Guterson." Even though I haven't seen him in years, I thank the one person whose teaching gave me the desire — and the hope — to follow in his footsteps. I fold up the letter and slip it into the envelope, but then I realize that I don't even know where he lives. So I address it "in care of Temple de Hirsch," where he taught me so long ago.

Later I discover that today's mail was loaded with hundreds of yellow envelopes, also delivering news to many of my classmates. Both Ric and Jim have been accepted by their first-choice East Coast law schools — no surprise, since both have terrific LSAT scores and excellent grades.

By dinner time, a nagging agitation is insisting that I call Mom, but I just can't bring myself to do it. Instead, with a new lightness, I walk to Stevenson for my evening shift. As I put on my white plastic apron, Cleve comes over and throws an arm over my shoulder.

"So, Hondo," he says, bending close to me, "got any news for me?"

"West Coast, Cleve," I smile. "Stanford."

"My man!" he smiles broadly, his bright white teeth beaming. "Knew you'd do it!" He claps me on the back. "Now get your skimpy ass out there and tell Caddy. Soon, you and me — we'll do some celebratin' over a good meal!"

175

When I tell Caddy the news, he embraces me. Then he steps back, looks me square in the face, and says gravely, "Now don't be putting on any airs, Bruce. You'd better hope there's a kitchen at Stanford where you can show off your *real* skills."

I'm bursting with affection for Cleve and Caddy. They've contributed so much to my success — but, just as I'm about to tell Caddy how grateful I am, he throws cold water on my warm feelings. "You called your mother yet?"

My expression tells him all he needs to know. He's heard about the fights we've had. Before I say anything, Caddy mutters under his breath, "I hope this damn war ends soon."

At 11 that night, I'm back in my room, finally facing the phone and what I should have done hours ago. It's 8 on the West Coast, and I reluctantly pick up the receiver and dial.

Mom picks up with her familiar "hello," and I feel myself stiffen. *Stop,* I tell myself. *She'll be thrilled. Don't anticipate problems...*

"I have good news," I forge ahead. "Really good news."

"Oh, well, I could certainly use some." Her bitter response is laden with the weight of years of loss and worry.

"Stanford accepted me!" I say buoyantly. "I'm going there this fall." I can't bring myself to say anything about the elephant in the room — 90.

Mom swallows hard, choking back her emotions. Silence envelops both of us. Then I hear muffled sounds; she must have put her hand over the receiver. Either she's hiding her emotions from me or she's telling my sisters, Cindy and Adrienne, who is now attending San Diego State University.

Finally, the muffled sounds lift and she says with genuine enthusiasm, "That's wonderful news, Bruce, though I'm not surprised. I'm proud of you. Your father would be proud, too."

176

I bask in her rare tenderness — but then she undercuts it: "We'll find a way to make sure you go to law school this fall."

"Mom!" That familiar irritation floods me, and just like that, I'm ready to fight again. This is exactly why I didn't want to call her.

"I know, I know. Enough already with the draft business," she says, using words I've often said to her. "But let me help you...let me help you get out of this *meshugas*. I get that it's your life, but I just don't understand why you won't let me do anything."

"I can't talk to you about —"

"I just wish this damn war would end already," she says with exasperation.

"I know, Mom." At least we can agree on that.

"This is a day of celebration, Bruce. Let's not let anything interfere with that."

"I appreciate that, Mom." Deeply relieved, I add, "More than you know. I'll call on Sunday night, when the rates go down. We can talk longer then.

"And, Mom," I hesitate before expressing my feelings — but then, I decide to just risk it: "I love you, Mom."

I know she's uncomfortable with emotion, always at a loss for any response. An awkward silence falls between us.

When she finally speaks, my miscalculation is confirmed. "Okay, we'll talk more on Sunday."

Late April 1971

"Selective Service, San Diego office. How may I direct your —"

"Mary Ann," I interrupt her professional voice, "it's me, Bruce... Bruce Wasser calling."

"Oh, hi there, Bruce. Haven't heard from you in a while. Everything OK?" Then a hint of anxiety creeps in: "You still in school?"

"Yes, and I have some good news, I think." I pause a moment before telling her about Stanford. Then — not wanting her to think I'm looking for special treatment — I quickly launch into the real reason I'm spending money on a long-distance call in the middle of a work week.

"Mary Ann, you told me to get some letters written on my behalf. So I've asked several people who know me pretty well. I even asked Coach Eiler, as you suggested. He told me he'd have one for you soon.

"And I told everyone not to just write about my beliefs, but also about my sincerity and my ideas. That's what the latest Supreme Court decision requires, right? That's what you wanted?"

Even as I hear myself ask, I realize her answer is irrelevant; the letters are in the mail already. If the board wants something else, I'm going to feel really awkward asking the same people to write a different letter.

"Yes, that's right," she says. "That's just what we need, Bruce."

I let out a sigh of relief.

"And Bruce, I need these letters as quickly as possible. Your deferment ends in a couple of months, and you want your file to be complete well before the board makes its decision."

The clock starts ticking again in my mind, as loud and insistent as ever. "And thanks again for your help —" I say.

"Oh!" Mary Ann jumps in before I can tell her how grateful I am for all her guidance. "And congratulations on law school!"

A rush of warmth runs through me as I bask in her approbation. "Th... thanks! Really appreciate —"

But she interrupts me again with a stinging clarification: "Now, let's just hope you get to go."

* * *

A few weeks later, I stack the copies of the letters that were sent to the draft board on my desk. They've arrived in my mail over the past few weeks. In addition, a few days ago, I received a pamphlet-sized reproduction of the Supreme Court's June 15, 1970, *Welsh v. United States* decision that I requested. I look through the pamphlet again, focusing on the passages I had underlined and highlighted. The details of this case will determine my future.

The Court's decision was far from unanimous, with only three justices joining the opinion written by Justice Black. Three others, including the Chief Justice, dissented. That leaves plenty of latitude for draft boards to deny non-religious applications.

Despite the Court's divisions, the decision states clearly that CO status is not dependent on religious beliefs; rather, "Religious training or belief" do include moral or ethical grounds. The key is proving sincerity, consistency, and depth of belief — and others must attest to the applicant's intangible, emotional, existential qualities, as required by *Welsh*.

Now, I turn my attention to the letters. Fearing what they'll say, I haven't been able to bring myself to read any of them. I collect the three that will carry the most weight: Jim Lieber, Professor Garvey, and Coach Eiler.

Confident that I can count on Jim, I read his letter first. It's one page, short and direct. Poignantly, he warns that, if I'm forced into military service, "A great deal of Bruce's idealism and ambition to serve would die. It would be America's loss."

I hadn't thought of it that way, but Jim is right: Defying my conscience would kill my desire to serve America in other capacities.

Professor Garvey's is the next one in my stack. Ever since we met at that freshman-year baseball game, Garvey has remained an enigma to me. When I asked him to write this letter, I worried whether his military experience would influence what he would say — not to mention his work in the presidential administrations of the early 1960s, including as an architect of the present war. I can't imagine that he'll write me a pass to get out of service.

My hands shake as I slowly read his four-page letter:

> "I have known Bruce Wasser as a student and as a close family friend for almost three years while at Princeton University. Never in my experience as a college teacher, have I met any person of such evidently strong and compelling moral convictions as Bruce. I cannot comment on the substance of his theological or 'religious' beliefs in the conventional sense. But I do know from long personal observation and discussion — often on a deeply personal and intimate level — the depth of his convictions."

I let out a sigh of relief. This is exactly what the Welsh decision requires, and what my application needs. But there's more — to my surprise:

> "It would also be seriously destructive...of the morale and discipline of any military organization in which Bruce was forced to serve. He is, in my opinion, incapable of functioning effectively in a context which is, to him, morally equivocal. ... I write this as a former professional military officer, a graduate of the first class (1959) of the US Air Force Academy. I would trust Bruce to any lengths as a friend, but would regard him as a hostile and upsetting element in any military outfit."

I don't know whether to be honored or insulted.

The last letter is from Coach Eiler. Recalling my notion that his letter of recommendation was what persuaded Princeton's Admissions Committee to offer me a precious spot in the class of '71, I wonder if, ironically, my future might again rest on Eiler's words.

But now, I'm terrified to read those words. I need him to advocate for me despite — maybe even because of — our deep differences. Whatever he thinks of my politics, he has to recognize my deep dedication, whether to our basketball team or to personal principles.

Sitting on the edge of my bed, I quickly scan Eiler's introductory comments, in which he establishes the context of our relationship.

> "My relationship with Bruce began in 1965 when he was a tenth-grade student at Clairemont High School in San Diego. Shortly thereafter, personal tragedy struck when his father died and he faced the responsibilities as the only man in the family with three women. The next three years were to establish our unique relationship. As his athletic coach, grade level counselor and friend, he asked of me and received whatever guidance was needed for a young man.

"During these years, Bruce related strong inner feelings about violence and war. Upon high school graduation and as each college year concluded, I saw a reinforced feeling against all war and related activities. I am convinced that now, [upon] graduation from college, he is totally and honestly a legitimate objector to... involvement in any war."

Again, I roll those words over in my mind: "totally and honestly a legitimate objector..." This, from the man who once said to me: "A patriot never questions authority. He does what's asked of him, without reservations."

As a mentor, friend, father figure — incredibly, once again, Eiler has given me exactly what I need. I swallow the lump in my throat as I consider how this man of deep principles has set aside his own strongest convictions to support my antithetical beliefs. In this act, he has modeled magnanimity and manhood.

I return to the page and read the last line of his letter. Eiler never interjects his own political views into his statement; instead, he focuses entirely on me, leaving no doubt that I am sincere:

"I have strong convictions to recommend and plead that extreme consideration be given to Bruce in receiving CO status."

MAY 1971

With only a few weeks remaining until graduation, most seniors are euphoric. But I dread leaving the people who have become a second family to me.

Ascending to the second floor of Dickinson Hall on this unusually warm day, I face my most difficult goodbye — to Martin Duberman. I just hope nobody knocks on his door and interrupts our final meeting. Lately Martin has looked preoccupied, more burdened than ever. I've been wondering what weighs on him.

"Bruce!" He opens the door, gesturing toward my usual seat, then settling into the chair behind his desk.

"I want to share some news with you that you're going to hear anyway. But I want it to come from me."

"You okay, Martin?" I panic immediately. Whenever an adult has "news" for me, I presume it's disastrous. "I mean, you're not sick, are you?"

"No, actually, Bruce, I'm better than ever," Martin smiles broadly. "I feel fantastic." I notice that he's no longer grimacing with unspoken worries. In fact, he looks downright youthful, his hair curling over his collar and his hands clasped comfortably on the edge of his desk.

"I'm leaving this place!"

I'm surprised but, sensing his relief, I guess I'm happy for him.

"It's not healthy for me to be here," he goes on. "Or for *others* like me."

Everyone knows that Martin is an academic pariah, an outcast in the History Department, subject to endless petty jealousies and envies. Unlike other professors, Martin didn't care to live on campus, instead keeping an apartment in Greenwich Village. His academic peers disapprove not only of his untraditional approach, but also of his second occupation as a playwright whose New York productions have been lauded as enthusiastically as his award-winning historical works.

Still, I never grasped how unhappy Martin was here. Assuming that most professors would covet a teaching position at Princeton, I thought departmental politics was just an irksome but inevitable part of the job. I never imagined that being a misfit could drive him out altogether.

During our farewell conversation, I utterly fail to realize that there's more to Martin's "misfit" status than departmental politics. He's speaking in code, testing whether I understand what "others like me" actually means.

Martin's truth finally dawns on me more than a year later, as I read his essay in a December 1972 issue of *The New York Times* book review section. The article is entitled "Homosexual Literature."

> "After months of reading the 'scientific' and 'movement' literature on homosexuality," Martin writes, "I'm convinced that no one is in possession of sufficient knowledge at this point in time (though almost no one concedes this) to warrant the confident generalizations heard on all sides — and especially on the scientific side. I write as one who has not only read the literature, but lived the life."

"Others like me" was a statement of his sexual orientation; he "lived the life" I knew nothing about. Shame surges through me as I realize that, back at Princeton, Martin was coming out to me — privately, long before his very public announcement. But I was too naive to be the friend he needed at that moment.

Now, Martin shares his plans — and a gift.

"I'll be teaching at Lehman College starting this fall, at the City University of New York," he says, and then briskly changes the subject. "But enough of this academic nonsense. I have something for you."

He stands, reaches over to an adjacent chair, and retrieves a wrapped parcel. "Open it, please."

I tear away the paper to find, in an elaborate old frame, an antique lithograph, its colors faded but still beautiful, titled "America."

Taken completely by surprise, I study the image, trying to sort out the meaning of its classical images.

In the foreground, a regal-looking woman warrior is seated under a palm tree. Her feather headdress suggests status, as does her weaponry: a large bow held in one hand and a quiver of arrows at her side both signal that she's prepared to fight, if necessary. She's pointing toward a menacing black rattlesnake coiled at her feet, flicking its forked tongue at an unseen enemy. Near the snake lies a slain pheasant, its claw still twisted around a scepter.

In the background, two innocent-looking children are approaching the woman. One child is holding a large fish — a symbol of abundance, I guess. Beneath the lithograph is the word "America," along with the publisher's name and the date it appeared: July 1, 1795.

"I want you to have this." Martin places a hand on my shoulder. "To make it part of your home, wherever you may live, on whatever path you take in life.

"This used to hang in my bedroom in Mount Vernon, New York, when I was a kid." Martin swallows, controlling his emotions. "As I see it, the goddess, 'America,' has fought for her country, and she's now at rest. But behind her emerge the children, the new generation, bearing, I think, the gifts of peace and prosperity."

I turn my gaze up to Martin, tears glazing my eyes. I'll treasure anything he chooses to give me, but this is much more than a picture to hang on my wall. With it, Martin is handing a baton to me and my peers, entrusting us with our nation's future.

"You are the new generation, Bruce." Martin pulls me toward him. I hug him tightly, drawing comfort and strength from his heartfelt embrace.

Then he speaks softly in farewell. "I hope America will receive the gifts you have in store for her."

* * *

That night, several of Martin's devoted fans gather in my room to create a special send-off for him. We apply our minimal artistic talents to creating a huge bed-sheet banner that we plan to unfurl from the balcony of McCosh 10, where Martin will deliver his final lecture.

A good half-hour before Martin arrives, the grand lecture hall is packed with current and former students, faculty, and staff. It's an eerie atmosphere — carnival-like, yet subdued, even despondent. Over the years, Martin has become an embodiment of youthful rebellion and a symbol of principled dissent.

Four of us stake out the middle of the first row of the balcony, excitedly gripping the folded bed sheet in our laps. I can't help but grin as I recall that two years ago, almost to the date, my roommate Chris and I pulled off one of the most infamous pranks in recent history. We disrupted a freshman English final by bursting into the room and staging a theatrical argument over my stealing Chris's girlfriend. We ended the dispute with Chris "shooting" me, the loud BANG of his toy gun startling the entire class. Bedlam ensued.

I'm not the same guy today, and, as the time for Martin's appearance nears, my stomach knots. I turn to a Stevenson friend sitting next to me and ask, "What do you think Martin will say today?"

"Not sure," he grins. "But I *know* we're gonna break the tension, my man."

As Martin enters the room and walks to the podium, the crowd falls silent. He looks down at his notes, adjusts his glasses, and characteristically runs his fingers through his hair.

The four of us jump to our feet and yell, "Hey, Martin!" We unfurl the crude banner that reads: "Without Marty, P'ton will be farty." He stares up at the balcony and bursts into laughter. Throughout the hall, heads turn up and back toward our proud statement. Loud peals of laughter erupt, followed by rhythmic clapping that gets picked up all over the room. Suddenly, it feels like we're sitting in Jadwin Gym during a tight basketball game. The audience starts a chant: "Mar-tin! Mar-tin! Mar-tin!"

The chorus doesn't abate, and Martin abandons his prepared remarks, walks away from the podium, and sits on the lip of the stage floor. For the next 45 minutes, he speaks extemporaneously, giving all of us a benediction — a blessing — sending us into our future with hope and renewed purpose.

Concluding with an injunction, he quotes from the poet Dylan Thomas: "Do not go gentle into that good night... Rage, rage against the dying of the light."

The audience springs to its feet for a standing ovation. Martin rises as well and leaves the hall for the last time.

* * *

Martin's departure from Princeton hollows me out. Though I really don't want to spend any more time here, I force myself to take my senior "comprehensive" examination. This ritual consists of writing an essay, then engaging in a dialogue with two professors. My assigned discussion — exploring the firing of shots at Fort Sumter, which triggered the Civil War — hardly needs further analysis. To me, "comps" are the pinnacle of Princeton pretension: exhausted, disengaged students posture before pompous professors who, after this final arcane rite, will grant us permission to graduate.

I'd argued with Martin about boycotting the entire charade, but he urged me not to throw away years of study and commitment. "Pick your battles," Martin advised. "Don't joust with windmills." Following his counsel, I show up unprepared, with a conspicuous lack of interest — and pass nonetheless.

In mid-May, I learn that I've been awarded Phi Beta Kappa honors. Yet, trudging to the reception for honorees, I feel so weary of Princeton. Even with flowers and trees in full bloom all over campus, everything looks different now. The Gothic buildings feel like a citadel of elitism and entitlement — the arches medieval, the iron gates imprisoning. Even the fabled "lofty elms" seem to be canopies shading cold cruelty.

Nothing tethers me here; I've had enough of Princeton's smug sense of privilege and elitist traditions. Then and there, I decide this will be my last ceremony at Princeton. Instead of attending graduation activities, or even the ceremony itself, I'm going to leave campus early and get on with my life.

* * *

ow I just have to share this decision with my mother, who has been impatiently awaiting information about attending my graduation. This will not be an easy call. I try to come up with the gentlest way to break the news to her, while summoning the strength to pick up the receiver and dial her number.

"Hi, Mom," I say to her "Hello."

Before I can say another word, she jumps in, breathless. "I'm so thrilled about your graduation. I've made plane reservations with open dates."

The pitch of her voice is much higher than usual. I haven't heard her sound so excited in years. "I need some information so I can secure my seats —"

"Mom," I try to cut her off. "Mom —"

"I don't know where I'll stay," she goes on. "But I'm sure you can work something out for me. Have any suggestions?"

"I... I'm not going to graduation," I blurt out.

"What? What did you say?" Her rage surges in those five words. Then she lapses into the familiar tone she uses when she hates a decision I've made. "You're telling me you're not going to attend your own *graduation?*"

"I'm just too unhappy here, Mom." I say, hoping to elicit her compassion. "I just can't. I want to come home and get ready to start my new job."

I've lined up a paid internship at the San Diego branch of the United States Federal Public Defender's Office. My supervisor, Robert Cleary, plans to use my ability to speak and write in Spanish to interview Spanish-speaking indigent defendants charged with a federal crime. I'm eager to finally contribute to legal cases and wrestle with real-world problems.

"Mom, I can't put into words how much I want to get out of here, and —"

"For four years, I have been looking forward to this." She's seething now. "Four years! You have been the hope of this family. Is this the thanks I get for raising you? For supporting you?"

Then she clobbers me with the most damning question she poses when she's furious: "What kind of son *are* you?"

I know I'm depriving her of real pleasure. My guilt makes me wonder if maybe I should stay another three weeks, if only to smooth over the damage I've done to our relationship. Why not give in?

Just as I'm asking myself this question, she comes at me with renewed fury. "You are so selfish, thinking only of what *you* want. How can you do this to *me?*"

Silence settles between us, and then she delivers her final punch. "I don't ask much of you, Bruce, but you're depriving both of us of so much. This is *wrong!*"

With a heavy sigh, she pauses for effect and then, finally, concedes: "Let me know when you're coming home. You can't see what you're doing now, but one day you'll regret this."

* * *

On my last day on campus, Ric and I sit down to our final breakfast together.

"It's weird," he says over our usual eggs and bacon. "I just can't believe we're not going to be doing this anymore, Jerome. I mean, how many years have we been meeting like this?"

"Uhh, let's see," I search my memory to remember what year this tradition started. "Spring semester sophomore year, I think. Right?"

"Sounds right. Every day! You realize that's probably over 500 breakfasts!"

We both let that number sink in; then Ric says, "You're gonna have a tough time finding someone at Stanford who'll get up at 6 in the morning to meet your sorry ass for breakfast. And nobody's gonna beat that record!"

"I'm sure I can find some fuck-up who'll fill your big shoes, Sheldon."

He laughs, and then adds, "I know I needle you — sometimes too much. But you know how I feel about you, Jerome."

"You have a strange way of showing it." I narrow my eyes at him, trying to anticipate his next remark.

"I don't mean half the shit I throw at you..." he looks at me with his usual mischievous grin. "Well, maybe a third.

"So! I had this great idea." He touches his temple. "What if we retire your white apron and hang it from the rafters at Stevenson? You'd be honored in the same way the Celtics retired the Couz or Loscutoff, with their numbers hanging in the Boston Garden."

"Ha!" I'll miss Ric and all the ways he makes me laugh. "Not sure that would have the same honor and weight. It would probably look like a dirty rag someone threw up there."

"Yeah," Ric nods. "Something tells me Caddy and Cleve probably won't go for it either."

We spend the rest of our breakfast chatting about law school and our summer plans. When we reluctantly get up from the table, we clasp each other's shoulders with great affection, not sure how to say good-bye.

Then Ric steps away and calls out the same words he has said so many mornings, as if this is just another day and we'll see each other tomorrow. "You're onto yourself, Jerome!"

*　*　*

Later in the day, I see Jim. We're planning to get together again soon, so that parting isn't too hard. But leaving the Garvey family, and Cleve and Caddy, will be much more emotional.

I slowly walk down Prospect Avenue to the Garveys' house, where I've continued to babysit nearly every Sunday for the past three years. I bite my lip, hard, when LuAnn hugs me and the kids proudly present me with a graduation card. Professor Garvey looks me squarely in the eye and says, "I'm not going to say good-bye, Bruce. I'm simply not going to. All of us — particularly my children — will miss you."

Then he says something opaque: given our political differences, I'm not sure what he means. "Don't ever give up on your country, Bruce. The stakes are too high." Does he think that I'm giving up on my country by becoming a CO? Is that some sort of judgment of me?

As always, Garvey is an enigma to me; fittingly, that is his parting shot.

I head over to the Stevenson kitchen, donning my usual white apron to work one last time as a dishwasher. I turn off the radio, preferring to listen to the hum of the familiar machinery and breathe in the humid, food-scented air around me. The clanging of the silverware is much louder when bass drums aren't drowning out the noise.

After the dinner shift ends, Cleve calls me over to his table. I see he has made my favorite treat as a sendoff: a little sweet potato pie, just for me.

Sitting down, I eagerly take a few bites, then look up at him gratefully. He nods, as if he's come up with the right answer to a question he's been asking himself.

Pointing his index finger at me, he says, "Don't forget this place, Hondo. You still got dues to pay, boy. You got dues to pay. Now — get out of here, and make me proud of your skimpy white ass."

I flash a smile, wave, and push open the kitchen door; for the last time, I let it swing shut behind me. In the Stevenson foyer, I see Caddy shaking hands with several students, saying his farewells.

I know he doesn't have much time to spend with any one of us. When I finally get his attention, I'm at a loss for words. So is he.

Caddy places his large palms on my shoulders, takes a long look at me, and then pulls me in close for a warm hug. He whispers in my ear the same thing he said to me nearly two years ago on the cold winter night of the lottery.

"Good luck, Bruce. Good luck."

Summer 1971

"So, what do you think of your job, Bruce?"

William Cleary, the head public defender in the United States Department of Justice Federal Defenders office, looks up from his grilled cheese sandwich and focuses his dark, penetrating eyes directly on me.

We're having lunch at a greasy spoon near our office in downtown San Diego. The informal diner always relaxes me; the sounds of the kitchen bring back the familiar, noisy comfort of Stevenson Hall.

"It's better than anything I could've imagined, Mr. Cleary." My response scarcely captures my thrill with the work of this internship. Joining the public defenders has absolutely confirmed my career choice: "I feel like I found what I want to do with my life."

"So wonderful for you." He smiles at me kindly. "You're at the beginning of what I'm sure will be a remarkable career."

"Thank you," I say — and then add, as if hedging my bets, "I hope so." Mr. Cleary has no idea, but those three loaded words capture my apprehension as I await word from the draft board.

"You know, our clients are unique... And challenging," Mr. Cleary, who is roughly twice my age, continues. "How do you find them?"

"They don't really seem to understand what's happening to them," I say. "A lot of the guys don't speak English. Some confuse me with *la migra*. They're worried I'm going to deport them."

"Yeah, that's a problem," he says. "They don't get that we're the good guys, and we're here to help."

"Some of them don't understand what it means to be an American," I nod. "They don't get the idea of 'rights.' They worry how they're going to pay me."

I've completely forgotten my cheeseburger and fries. "Even after I've told them that we're working for them, without cost, they keep asking me about my bill."

Cleary, a muscular, short man, points to my plate, reminding me to eat. Since I started working for him two weeks ago, I've seen that he's both idealistic and coldly realistic. His appearance shouts "conservative" — crew cut, charcoal-gray suit, American flag pin on his lapel — but I already know otherwise. He doesn't talk progressive politics; instead, he lives by his belief that change is possible only by working within the system.

"Look, Bruce," he says, after taking a sip of his lemonade. "You and I both know that most of these men are probably guilty. They either knowingly or unknowingly broke federal laws... Immigration, drugs, human trafficking.

"Don't be deceived. They see you as a mark — some dumb white kid they can con. They'll feed you any line of bullshit to see if you'll swallow it. Some of them are genuine bottom feeders.

"But that's why I'm here, and why you're here, too: We believe they still have rights. They are up against the most powerful government in human history, a government that has incredible resources to make them criminals, to brand them as worthless for the rest of their lives. They're indigent, but that doesn't mean they're less deserving of full protection of the law."

His darting eyes and forceful gestures emphasize his passionate beliefs. At one point in his monologue, his hand grazes a glass of water, nearly tipping it over.

"They — more than almost anyone else charged with a crime — need the very best defense possible," he continues, although he doesn't need to convince me. "The *best!*"

I stop eating again and look across the scarred old table at Mr. Cleary. He reminds me of my Sunday school teacher, Mr. Guterson — level-headed, conscience-driven, utterly dedicated. Already, he is much more than a boss to me.

"Mr. Cleary," I admit, "I'm far from the best. I'm green, probably terribly naive, and I have a lot to learn. But the reasons I'm here are the same as yours. I can't wait to wake up in the morning and get to work!"

He smiles knowingly, and I suspect he sees in me his younger, driven self. He has even indicated that I can look forward to a future with him: "You'll be a great asset to us," he said about a week ago.

But there are things I can't tell Mr. Cleary. If I say it out loud, it would become too real, too crushing. I'm so afraid I'll never get the chance to go to law school, never be admitted to the bar, never have the opportunity to serve alongside Mr. Cleary.

If my CO application fails, I'll have to refuse induction, and *I'll* be the one charged as a criminal, branded for life as an Un-American felon.

* * *

"Mom! Come here!" One day in late June, arriving home from work, I pick up a cylindrical tube and a cardboard box that the mailman left on the front stoop. Both are addressed to me, postmarked Princeton, NJ Rubber-banded to the parcels is a thin, official-looking letter from the United States Selective Service, San Diego.

"Mom! I've got some things you'll want to see."

In the kitchen, Mom is checking on her casserole in the oven. She stops what she's doing, sets down her potholders, and perches next to me at the table.

"This is so exciting," I say. "I've been waiting so long for all this."

Mom doesn't even object when I grab her paring knife to pry off the cap on the tube. Without ceremony, but very gently, I pull out my rolled-up diploma. Spreading it out on the table, we both take a long look.

The diploma is embossed with Princeton's logo, signed by the university president, and augmented with a gold label, announcing that I graduated with distinction in history. Also tucked into the cylinder are two more modest certificates, recognizing my participation in the Afro-American Studies Program and my selection as a member of Phi Beta Kappa. No matter how I feel about my time at Princeton, I achieved the highest possible academic honors there.

Eyes fixed on the table, Mom picks up the kitchen towel hanging on the back of a chair, wiping her hands to make sure they're clean. Tossing the towel over her shoulder, she pushes my hands away from the diploma and certificates. They snap back into a tight roll, which she then unfurls again.

Spreading the papers on the table, she first secures the diploma's corners: the salt shaker, the pepper shaker, the napkin holder, the butter dish. Then she holds the two certificates open, one hand on each. Looking from one to the next, she closely examines my accomplishments.

She picks up the towel, covers her eyes with it, and starts to cry.

I lower my head, not knowing what to say or do. Nervously, I stuff my hands under my legs as she composes herself. I've rarely seen her this emotional. I'm not even sure why she's crying.

"This would have been so much better if you had stayed," she moans. "So much better if you received this onstage. Accepted congratulations from all your professors. Shaken the president's hand."

"Mom," I plead, "let's not rehash this. Please. Try to savor this wonderful moment. The ceremony isn't important. What really matters is that I earned these honors."

She waves her hand, and then points at the unopened rectangular box. "What's that?"

"I have no idea." Pushing it toward her, I offer, "Here, Mom, you can open it." I'm hoping to distract her from her sadness.

She extracts *The Nassau Herald '71*, a hardbound yearbook. "Oh, I almost forgot," I tell her. "Last fall, all the seniors had their pictures taken, and we wrote short sketches about ourselves. Check the back of the book for the Ws."

As if she were opening a birthday present, she hurriedly thumbs through the pages, searching for the index so she can locate me. But, first, she stumbles upon the "Senior Class Poll — 1971."

"What's this?" Focusing intently, she scours the poll. "Do you think you're mentioned?"

"Who cares? I wasn't into class politics. That poll is probably like those stupid lists in high-school yearbooks that tell you about graduating classmates. Don't bother with it, Mom. Let's find my picture."

"Hmmm," she murmurs, her eyes scanning down the poll.

"I'm trying to remember... I'm not sure I even combed my hair for that photograph."

Then she gasps, and I feel her deflate instantly, like a balloon.

"Mom, what's wrong?"

"Explain *this* to me!" She points accusingly to page 427, which features a list identifying certain seniors' defining characteristics. "Most Brilliant" is, of course, the classmate who everyone knew was a genius.

But what caught Mom's eye was the line directly beneath "Most Brilliant."

"Thinks He Is: Wasser."

It's a sucker punch the likes of which I've never felt.

Those four words contain all the suffering I endured in my years at Princeton. From matriculation to graduation, I never fit in. I knew it; they knew it, too.

Now, this snide, scornful summary of my Princeton experience is recorded in black and white. Right here, in the yearbook, for all my classmates to see and remember. I'm mortified and humiliated, but also relieved: I never have to set foot on that campus again!

"Why would someone do this?" Mom shakes her head in confusion.

"Sorry you had to see it." I take the book from her hands and close it, as if that will erase what she just read. Those cruel words will sting for a long time, but at this moment, I try to minimize the insult by reassuring my mother — and myself. "It doesn't mean anything."

"*This* is how they send off a classmate?" She's still shaking her head in disbelief. "Why would they say this?"

"I tried to tell you... That place was never right for me," I say. "No matter how hard I tried, I couldn't make it work. That's why I wanted to come home as soon as I could. Now do you understand, Mom?"

"Not really," she says, as she picks up the last envelope and hands it to me.

"Here's the answer to my future," I say. "You ready for this, Mom?"

"I guess I'm ready, but I think I'll leave the kitchen while you open it. I can't take any more bad news."

Hands shaking, heart pounding, I carefully slice the seal and remove a tissue-thin slip of paper. In simple language, above the signature of the Executive Director of the San Diego Draft Board, the 3-by-5-inch document announces my status:

Selective Service System
Notice of Classification
This is to certify that
Bruce Jay Wasser
Selective Service No.
4-141-49-1098
is classified in Class 1-O

1-O! That's government code for conscientious objector!

"Mom, come here!" I yell in a high pitch. *"Mom!"*

She comes charging back into the kitchen as I shout, "I'm a CO! I did it. I made it."

"So what does that mean, Bruce? How does that change things?"

I'm staring at the tiny certificate that I've coveted — obsessed over — for so long. Preoccupied by this enormous shift in my identity, I can't be bothered right now to answer Mom's persistent questions.

"Can you go to law school?" she presses.

I am 1-O. Officially.

I'm still 90, but now I know I'm not going to jail. Instead, when I'm called up, I'll do alternative service work.

Now, in an instant, 90 is just ...well, it's just 90 again. A two-digit number, useful only for counting and measuring. It no longer holds power over me.

I add this plain, priceless slip of paper to the spread of gold-sealed honors on the kitchen table. This accomplishment means as much to me as all of my Princeton distinctions.

"But what about law school?" My mother repeats, and finally gets my attention. "Can you still go?"

"Mom, I need to pass a physical, probably in a few weeks." I'm laying out my plans for both of us to assess. "Then, after finishing up at the public defender's office, I'll try to get a job around Palo Alto to fulfill my 1-O status."

"Palo Alto?" Mom asks suspiciously. "The Bay area? Are you taking *her?*" Mom is referring to the woman I've been going with for the past three years. I don't like the dismissive tone of her voice, but it's better than what she usually calls my girlfriend — "the *shiksa.*"

"Mom." I'm struggling to keep the conversation on track. "I know how you feel, but this has nothing to do with her. The Bay Area is a lot more liberal and anti-war than San Diego, so I think I'll have an easier time finding alternative service work there."

Tapping her finger impatiently on the slip of paper that grants me CO status, she asks again, "But what about law school, Bruce?"

"I'll visit Stanford when I'm in the area. I'll meet with the dean and get my admission deferred to 1973."

"Really?" She looks skeptical. "You think it'll be that easy?"

I clench my teeth, as I always do when she annoys me. Doesn't she have any understanding of what it took to get that 1-O next to my name? Of what this *means* to me? No matter what I say or do, it always feels like she's dumping cold water on my plans — and on me.

"Mom, it's just a formality," I shrug. "A deferral is no big deal. It's just a temporary detour on my way to Stanford. Don't worry!"

She shakes her head, side to side, first slowly, and then, like a locomotive, gaining speed and strength.

"I don't think so." Narrowing her eyes at me, she seems to see things I don't.

"Mom, why are you always so negative? Why can't you —"

"Don't be so sure of yourself." With a snap, she cuts me off. "Nothing... *nothing* is guaranteed when it comes to this CO business."

* * *

Later in the week, I visit the Selective Service office, to thank Mary Ann Blaum for all her help. As soon as I push open the door, she greets me with a large smile. Dropping her usual formal manner, she gets up from her chair, steps around her desk, and greets me by holding out her hand to shake mine.

Mary Ann's big grin isn't the only sign that things have changed in the three years I've known her. A few more wrinkles have set in at the sides of her eyes, and her hair is streaked with gray. I'm sure I look older, too; after all, I first walked into this office as a nervous, unformed 19-year-old. Mary Ann has watched me transform from a late-adolescent boy into a young man.

I suspect, too, that the war has taken a toll on both of us. As the public face of the San Diego draft board, Mary Ann doesn't have an easy job.

"I want to tell you something, Bruce," she says as she walks back around her desk and settles into her chair. "But I really couldn't, until now. It's about the board's decision."

For a brief second, I worry that she's going to tell me my 1-O status is in jeopardy. But that doesn't make sense, given her warm and friendly manner today.

She shuffles through some papers on her desk, finds a specific file, and opens it. "Over a year ago," she begins, "I began to intercede on your behalf. Of course, I couldn't let you know anything about that."

"Intercede?" I'm surprised and confused. "What exactly did you do?"

"You know," she explains, "most applicants don't realize it, but we clerks have a good deal of power over the board. They are very busy men, and they depend on us to weed out weak or false claims."

"Oh, I wondered about that," I say, "but I wasn't sure." I'd never let on that my dad had alerted me to the power of secretaries. Instead, I revert to my usual deferential, worried disposition: "I thought you might be annoyed at me because I was so slow with my letters of support."

She gently waves her hand at me, and I notice the bracelets she's wearing have a stylish, counterculture look.

"Bruce, we get a lot of boys who are truly scared about enlistment, but who aren't genuine objectors. Some don't even take the time to make a comprehensive argument. Others copy letters from other CO applicants."

Leaning forward a little, she continues. "I did some research on you, and on your unique circumstances. So when I told our board members, 'He's for real!' — I was confident. I told them that you did everything I asked, and I've never met a young man more worried about doing right. I told them, 'He is as sincere as they come.'"

Now she leans back, satisfied with the result she helped bring about. "So — congratulations! You are the *first* man to be granted conscientious objector status on non-religious grounds in this draft board's history. And in a military town like San Diego, that's saying something!"

I've long felt I have a special connection with Mary Ann, but I never thought she would have this much influence on my application. I never imagined she would go to bat on my behalf.

"Thank you, Mary Ann!" But those words don't begin to express appreciation. I try again. "Thanks. I'll never forget what you've done. I'm indebted to you."

She gazes at me across her plain old desk that, to me, once symbolized the steep, solid wall of the government itself. The wall seemed to be insurmountable, but now I see that Mary Ann gave me the boost I needed — all under Tricky Dick's watchful eyes.

"You deserve this status, Bruce." Her smile warms me as much as her life-changing kindness. "You worked hard for it, and you showed me — showed all of us — that you are a man of strong convictions."

On a sweltering July morning, I'm waiting to board a bus in downtown San Diego to travel to Long Beach, a suburb of Los Angeles, for my draft physical. San Diego is still considered a small city, dwarfed by its sprawling neighbor some 120 miles north. And, despite its deserved reputation as a military town, San Diego lacks the institutional infrastructure to process draftees. So Long Beach is our destination.

It's 6 a.m.; the sun is just rising. Most of us are disheveled and groggy, having rolled out of bed and thrown on T-shirts and shorts to get here on time.

Dissidents crowd the bus station, surrounding the 200 draftees as we board the buses. The protestors carry signs bearing slogans like "Pull Out Dick, Like Your Father Should Have" as they chant the familiar anti-war mantra: *"All we are saying... is give peace a chance."*

I identify with the protestors, but they definitely don't identify with me. To them, anyone boarding a bus to join the military is acquiescing to the evil system they're denouncing — even though everybody here was drafted. For me, it's an eerie, mortifying experience to be perceived as pro-war.

I climb on the bus, grab a window seat, and gaze out at the wild gathering, surprised that so many protesters got up so early to rail against the inductees' buses. Suddenly, out in the crowd, I spot a familiar face: Donnie Martin, one of my basketball teammates at Clairemont! His protest sign bears the classic exhortation: "Drop Acid, Not

Bombs." What a change, I think. When he was warming the bench with me in 1967, he was a chubby kid sporting a buzz-cut. Now, his reddish-brown hair hangs down his back and his lean body radiates energy. As he squints and scans the bus windows, I don't know whether to wave at him or duck.

Some of the guys doze off even before the bus rumbles onto the freeway. By 8:30 or so, we're parked in front of the Long Beach Seventh Street Armory, an austere, white-tiled building that takes up a couple of city blocks and looks like a prison.

Snarling military men greet us harshly as we disembark. "Groups of twenty! *Twenty!* Can't you count?" The inductees scurry around chaotically, bumping into each other, all of us strangers trying to organize ourselves into groups.

I approach a few stragglers drifting together toward the building. "You with them?" I ask. When nobody responds, I join them as my "group of twenty," assembling with the others in the large entryway.

"Many of you fuck-ups are here trying to get out of serving," booms a sergeant with a rigid bearing. His muscles bulge from his white shirt, which bears a set of gold stripes; his hair is no more than 1/16 of an inch long.

"Others of you," he looks around contemptuously, "are too damn dumb to know your heads from your asses. Don't try any funny shit with us. We've seen it all.

"Just do what we tell you. Don't ask dumb-ass questions. Just keep your fuckin' mouth shut and say, 'yes, sir,' or 'no, sir' to whatever we ask. You hear me? 'Yes, sir,' or 'no, sir!'"

I already feel assaulted; these men remind me vividly that I could never stomach this abusive culture. Later I learn that they're non-commissioned officers, themselves humiliated by being assigned to this "shit detail."

"We're gonna make sure *all* of you pass your physicals." His growl is a threat, not a promise.

Clearly, the officers and the inductees have drastically different goals. Some of these guys will do anything to flunk their physicals and get out of serving; meanwhile, the military are hell-bent on making *all* of us acceptable recruits.

"If you fuck up on this test," the sergeant adds ominously, "we'll keep your sorry ass here overnight till you pass."

Then he guides my group into a large classroom, where 100 of us are to take an "aptitude" test. Sliding into a school desk, I glance through the booklet we've been given. On its pages are several simple yet mysterious mechanical drawings. To me, they all look like hieroglyphics.

Paging through the booklet, staring at the puzzling images, I find that nothing penetrates my foggy brain. It appears that the questions — more illustrations than words — were designed for inductees with little education, even those who don't speak English, to figure out by deciphering the diagrams. Still, nothing here makes any sense to me.

I manage to determine that the test is presenting schematics of machines, and the questions apparently are asking how to assemble them. "How do you flip this on/off switch?" "How does item A fit into item B to assemble this part?" "When is it necessary to use a washer with a screw?" Turning to the back of the booklet, I find the more difficult questions are even worse: "What does RPM mean?" "How does a piston work in an engine?" "What does a carburetor do?"

The test is multiple choice, but I can't even hazard a guess. My Princeton education means absolutely nothing here. Sweat soaks my shirt.

Suddenly, I notice pages rustling and pencils scratching loudly at the desks all around me. Other guys are racing through the test as if it presents no challenge. One by one, they pop up from their desks to submit their filled-in Scantron answer sheets to the sergeant. Over and over, they distract me, pricking my feelings of intimidation and growing terror.

Now, for the first time, I know how it feels to struggle hopelessly with an incomprehensible subject.

Grinding my teeth, I see there's less than an hour left to finish. What if I really can't pass this test? Will they think I deliberately failed? Could I be arrested? Would they send me to a military psychologist? Who knows what will happen to me there?

"Concentrate!" I tell myself, trying to shut out these panicky thoughts. As the minutes tick away, I flip through the booklet, back and forth, searching for some easy question I understand. But I find only a few; everything else looks like a complex mathematical equation, far beyond my ability to solve. My mind is frozen.

Finally, in desperation, I decide to ask the sergeant for help. I know he wants us to pass, so maybe he'll give me some direction.

"Sir," I begin, leaning over to whisper and show him my booklet. "I don't understand these questions. I don't know anything about machinery, and I can't even make educated guesses. Can you help me out?"

"What?" Jaw clenched, he looks up and squints while pulling away from me, as if stupidity were contagious. "You some college boy? Don't know shit from Shinola about the real world! What the fuck they teach you at those snobby-ass places?"

"Sir," I say quietly, "I *need* to pass this test. I... I'm..." I stop, not sure what to tell him. I doubt he'll be sympathetic, but I don't have much choice. So I tell him the truth. "I... I'm a conscientious objector, sir, and I *want* to serve..."

"Conscientious objector!" He spits the words with contempt; this, obviously, is far worse than stupid. "And you want me to *help* you? Why?"

"Please, sir." I'm begging now. "I can barely think straight and, unlike everyone else here, I *want* to pass the test. I *have* to pass so I can do my alternate service."

"Alternate service," he mutters, shaking his head in disgust. It's the exactly same reaction I've seen so often: people see me as Un-American or worse. "Fuckin' coward," he seethes.

Then he looks at the booklet to see what questions have stumped me. Clearly, he has no compassion — but, I remind myself, he can't change my status. To him, I'm a problem someone else can deal with; he just wants me out of his hair. If I don't pass, I'll disrupt his process, and the last thing he wants is what military men call a SNAFU – Situation Normal All Fucked Up.

So, rolling his eyes with utter disdain, he points to the answers to several questions.

"Thank you," I whisper fervently. His guidance clears my head and, when I return to my seat, I'm able to answer a few of the questions on my own.

Finally, with the hour almost up, the sergeant and I are the last two people in the room. When I glance at him, he's glaring at me. "Time's up," he barks, "hand in your test *now*."

Quickly filling in the remaining bubbles as I stand, I walk to the sergeant's desk and offer him my answer sheet. In return, without even looking at me, he hands me a sack lunch. His icy reproach and the stress of this ordeal leave me with no appetite for its contents: a cold, dry turkey on white, accompanied by a scrawny, bruised apple.

Soon I join the others in a different room for another battery of tests. These are physical exams, presumably to determine our fitness for service.

My group enters a large locker room, where we're told to take off all our clothes. Standing at a urinal, shoulder to shoulder with at least fifty other semi-naked men, I'm shocked to learn what some of my fellow inductees have done to themselves to get out of serving.

"Shit, man, I took a handful of salt tablets before I came here," one says. "That should give 'em some fucked-up numbers in my piss. I heard that's the ticket out."

"No! Not gonna work," another tells him. "They're on to that type of shit. If you want to get 4-F'ed, you gotta show them some kind of deformity. Some kinda weird shit happening in your body."

"That's right," another says. "I got drunk a couple weeks ago and had my buddy cut up my legs. Take a look, man." Several of us twist ourselves to look down at the deep slashes on the back of his calves. "Don't back away," he says when he sees our horror. "Yeah, that's right, they're gonna think I'm suicidal. Who wants that kind of freak in the military?"

The guy next to me, who hasn't said anything, shakes off the last drop of pee and turns to me. "I got my old man to talk to his doctor. Pretty sure he hates the war as much as me, so he wrote a letter saying I have 'collapsing veins.' That oughta get me outta this shit. How about you, man?"

I turn to him and mumble, "My mom tried to get me out of this any way she could. I fought her over everything."

"Are you fuckin' crazy, man?" my neighbor says. He probably thinks I'm some sort of gung-ho G. I. Joe.

"Nah, man. Just trying to do things my own way, that's all. Hope things work out for you, though."

214

Having heard the other inductees' ploys, the guy next to the slasher announces: "Y'all are stupid. No need to go to extremes. I'm claiming I'm queer." Twirling his hips, he sing-songs, "I'd rather be a *fag* than come home in a body *bag*."

Laughter erupts, prompting a drill sergeant to scream, "Stop the bullshit! Get your bare asses over here."

The physical exams are mortifying — even dehumanizing — and all are conducted out in the open, without any privacy. Like auto parts on an assembly line, we inductees line up, silently waiting our turn to be handled.

At the first station, I offer the doctor my paper. He takes it in one hand and, with the other, suddenly shoves a gloved finger up my ass. A shock wave runs through me, like an electrical current. Stunned, I instantly feel my body no longer belongs to me. He stamps my document indifferently as I reel from this invasion.

"Next," he shouts, without even looking up. I move on, trying to recover, fearing what's next.

At the second station, an orderly drops down to my privates with some sort of magnifier. I dread what torture he has in store. I shift uncomfortably on my feet, and he barks at me to stand still as he carefully inspects my nut sack.

Normally I'm not self-conscious, but this makes me edgy and inhibited. "Cough!" he says while taking a good, long look at everything. Then he bangs his stamp on my paper. "Next."

When an orderly hands me a plastic container and tells me to use it in the bathroom, I'm confident I can manage to comply. Peeing in a bottle at the crowded urinal — even in front of all the other inductees — is probably the day's only test I can pass without asking for help or begging for mercy.

At last, at the end of the long day, the sergeant calls out the names of a dozen "sorry-asses" who have to stay overnight until they pass:

"... Stone, Turner, Vine, Waller, Wilson..."

When I hear Wilson, my heart jumps. I've passed all my tests!

Finally, at 6:30, the draftees are discharged from the forbidding building, hooting and hollering like school kids breaking out for recess. As I trot to the bus, my head throbs and my stomach churns from the stress of this taste of boot camp. I'm sick of being tested, poked, prodded, and yelled at for ten hours straight.

I sniff the bus exhaust and hear the loud rumbling of the motor, taking unusual pleasure in these signs of normality. As I stumble up the steps onto the Greyhound, I can still feel that finger stuck up my ass. I grab the first open seat toward the front — the better to get off this bus first and fast.

With a long sigh of exasperation, I throw myself onto the worn, torn seat. Then, I glance out the window at the massive armory, relieved that I'll never again set foot in that house of horrors.

September 1971

By Labor Day of 1971, the Selective Service has reached the number 75 in the draft lottery. Those of us with 90 are sure to receive an induction notice by late October or early November.

I quickly find work in a laboratory at the Palo Alto Veterans Administration Hospital, under the auspices of Stanford University. My Princeton education may have prepared me for law school, but it was my dishwashing job at Stevenson Hall that trained me for my alternative service. In the VA lab, I'll be washing glassware for two years.

Now, all I need is for Stanford to defer my admission and guarantee my spot for the 1973 academic year.

I'm confident this won't be a problem. I read an article about the Law School's recently appointed dean, reporting that he plans to devote his energy to learning about the needs and thoughts of students. According to the article, he wants to talk and listen to anyone at the Law School. Certain he'll be sensitive to my situation, I make an appointment to meet with him and wrap up the details of deferring admission for two years.

As I enter the dean's large office on a cloudy September day, I notice the neatly framed diplomas arranged on the walls and the rows of legal books lined up in the floor-to-ceiling shelves. A heavy, leather-bound legal dictionary sits on a wooden stand at a large window offering an expansive view of the campus. Glancing out the window,

I realize that if it weren't for the red-tiled roofs topping the traditional university buildings, I could be gazing out at Princeton; this California campus has the same serene beauty and Ivy League feel.

Despite the striking resemblance, I can't wait to begin my studies here — my last step toward fulfilling my lifelong goal of becoming a civil rights attorney. The dean, too, could be a Princeton man: in his late 30s, hair conventionally styled, brown sideburns just long enough to suggest that he's slightly rebellious. Yet he looks very East Coast in his conservative gray suit and bow tie.

Taking a seat in a small wooden chair, I watch him busily shuffling papers and signing documents on his desk. For what seems like an awfully long time, I wait for him to acknowledge me.

"Hello, Mr. Wasser," he finally mutters, without even looking up at me.

What a strange, cold greeting! But I'm sure he's a busy man and wants to resolve my issue in short order. All he needs to do is sign off on my deferral, and he can get on with his day.

"Let's get to the bottom line," he says gruffly.

"Bottom line?" I shake my head in confusion. "I... I was hoping... I just wanted to talk to you about deferring my admission for two years while I do my alternative —"

"Yes, I'm aware." He cuts me off; then, grim-faced and businesslike, he adds dismissively, "I know all about it."

"Oh... you do?"

"The bottom line is that Stanford Law School, unfortunately, will not automatically grant you admission to the class of 1976." He delivers this news as if he's reading the rules and regulations from some Stanford Law School manual.

"Pardon me, Dean." My mind is short-circuiting; I'm trying hard to understand what he's saying. "Does that mean... are you saying that I can't defer my admission?"

"Yes, that's exactly what I'm saying." His icy tone sends shivers through me.

I feel like I've been kicked in the gut, but I try not to show emotion. For a few moments, we stare at each other in silence from opposite sides of his massive oak antique desk.

Then, to lessen the tension, he throws me a bone. "We encourage you to re-apply for admission at the appropriate time." Sounds like he's reading another line from his rule book.

"Apply again?" Now I can't keep my emotions in check; my angry tone and blazing eyes scorch him. "I don't see why that's necessary."

"Simply put," he says brusquely, "you don't fall into any of our categories for re-admission."

"Categories? What are your categories?"

Then it finally hits me: My military status must be the reason Stanford won't defer my admission. I hear my mother's voice: "Nothing... *nothing* is guaranteed when it comes to this CO business." She tried to warn me, but I dismissed her, assuming that deferring my admission was just a bureaucratic technicality.

"If you were an active member of the armed services," the dean drones, "if you were in the Peace Corps, if you were in VISTA, if you were a divinity student, if you were in the military — you would qualify. Your status does not fall into any of our categories."

"So what I'm hearing — what I think you're saying — is that because I'm a conscientious objector, you won't guarantee my spot in the class of 1976?"

"Yes, that's exactly what I'm saying." Firmly sticking to official policy, he adds, "You don't qualify for re-admission based upon our categories."

"But I'm doing my compulsory national service."

"I'm aware of your circumstances," he says flatly.

"But, Dean, please consider who I am." I switch to pleading with him, trying to sound reasonable and lawyerly. "I'm a good American. I'm not shirking my responsibilities to the United States. I'm doing alternative military service; I'll even be working for Stanford, in the VA hospital just down the road from here. How can you tell me I don't fit into your 'categories'?"

He doesn't answer. Instead, he returns to the stack of papers on his desk. When he finds something of compelling interest, he picks up his pen again.

"This isn't fair!" I snap.

My heart is pounding; blood courses through me; I'm burning with rage. I've worked so hard to get here. I excelled in all my classes at Princeton. I took the LSATs, wrote the essays, got the letters of recommendation. All so that I would be allowed to study in this place, my first-choice law school. I jumped through every Selective Service hoop — research, applications, testaments to my character, everything — to become San Diego's first non-religious CO.

And now, Stanford Law School is punishing me for abiding by my own moral code? For being a conscientious objector?

With clenched teeth, I growl at the dean. "How can you do this?"

Silence. He doesn't look up from his desk.

"It's not right!" I'm surprised to hear myself shouting. "This is a *law* school — one of the finest in America. What about fairness? What about due process? What about equal justice?"

"I'm sorry," he says hollowly, standing to indicate that our meeting is over. "There's nothing I can do for you."

Seething with anger, I bolt up, out of the skimpy chair.

Then I pick up the chair, slam it to the floor, and stomp toward the door.

But before I leave, I turn around to glare at him — not sure what I'll say or do.

"This is a *horseshit* decision," I yell.

Startled, the dean turns to stone: a statue behind his traditional lawyer's desk. Probably trying to remember how to call security.

"And you're a horseshit *coward* for enforcing it."

Then I slam the door on Stanford Law School.

September 1971 - September 1973
Alternative service

In my narrow, windowless "office" in the research wing of the Palo Alto Veterans Administration Hospital, I spend my days staring into a stinking, murky vat of syrupy liquid. This ferocious muck — a Coca-Cola-colored concoction of concentrated sulfuric acid and chromium dioxide — is formulated to remove protein from glass beakers, cylinders and petri dishes. After this initial cleaning, these items are placed in a sleek, powerful dishwashing machine. The final step is sterilization in a modern autoclave.

I'm performing my alternative service in a medical-research laboratory as a glassware washer. My job consists of menial, repetitive work, with a considerable element of danger and a lot of down time. Because the glassware needs to spend four hours soaking in the muck, I'm often faced with long stretches during which I have little to do but talk to coworkers and contemplate my cloudy future.

The liquid itself is terrifying; an errant splash of chromic acid could blind me. Every drip burns straight through my clothing and lacerates my skin. Just inhaling the fumes instantly jolts me to a higher level of focus. Instruments often fall into the vat, and I can't pick them up without exposing my skin to the acid. There's a pair of flimsy metal tongs, but they're too short to fish out anything without dipping a gloved hand into the toxic stew.

Some days, I feel like I'm facing down a raging dragon that spits fire at me every few minutes. When it lands, I jump back from the scorching cauldron and yell, "Fuck!" Startled, my coworkers stop whatever they're doing and call out, "You okay?" or "Call the burn unit!" In time, they get used to my cries; they know it's just part of the job. Eventually, they tease me about the great upside to the deadly splashing: at last I'm fashionable, with all my clothes, especially my pants, faded, shredded, and riddled with holes.

The four doctors who supervise me are all young, all driven to succeed. This haughty quartet seems to view me like their beakers: invisible, disposable, easily replaceable. Unintentionally but immediately, I got off on the wrong foot with them, possibly because their research is utterly incomprehensible to me. I've often wondered if they resent my Princeton education or if they're furtive hawks who detest my CO status. Whatever the reason, not one has spoken a word to me beyond clipped demands for glassware and corrections to my behavior.

In this barren place, I am not permitted to decorate my space. No photos, family or otherwise; no newspaper clippings, no cartoons, nothing. I'm not allowed to have a radio, and when one of the doctors hears me whistling some golden oldie like "Hello, Mary Lou" or "Satisfaction," he'll abruptly stop working to glare at me. Evidently, in some strange battle of the bands, my whistling competes with the classical music they play all day long.

"Mr. Wasser," one snapped recently, "this is a hospital! Act like you're in one."

"Kiss my rosy red ass," I think. But I need this job, so instead of retorting, I mumble some sort of obligatory apology.

During my first few weeks here, I tried to persuade the doctors to provide elbow-length gloves, rather than the inadequate wrist-length ones I'm given. Even when I showed them my bracelet of blistering burns, they just shrugged.

Every physician swears to follow the Hippocratic Oath, which requires them to "do no harm." These doctors' refusal to provide me with better gloves, goggles, or any necessary protective gear literally adds insult to injury. Their indifference to suffering caused directly by their negligence betrays their oath and feels like some arbitrary punishment.

As the days grind on, I realize that my employers do not care about me in the slightest. The doctors scarcely know I exist; no one ever offers a kind word for the dirty, dangerous work I do. This place is far more than a continent away from Stevenson Hall. There, my labor was just as menial, but at least I didn't leave work burned and blistering. Caddy made me feel respected and valued, and I never finished a shift without a stomach full of Cleve's home cooking. Here, I'm just one of the millions of Americans who toil every day at repetitive, boring, soul-crushing jobs.

This, I now understand, is the essence of labor for the "workers of the *real* world."

* * *

The highlight of my days is my breaks — especially lunch — and my occasional encounters with my coworker and best friend at the lab, Rocky McGill. Having worked here since the research wing first opened ten years ago, Rocky is probably the most valued lab tech in the place. He knows all the doctors and their idiosyncrasies. He also has a knack for imitations that unfailingly lighten this dreary place.

"Now, Mr. Wasser," he often chides me, feigning a British accent to mock one of the doctors. "If you're going to engage in this kind of behavior, please, please, please... oh, drat it all... I can't even find the *words* to let you know how *disappointed* I am in you."

His impersonations crack me up every time. A short, stocky Black man in his early 30s, Rocky sports a spectacular 'fro that adds a good five inches to his height. He often whips out his black pick from the back pocket of his jeans and goes to work, touching it up here and there to make sure he maintains maximum volume. Meanwhile, peering up and over his aviator glasses, he quietly schools me in the politics of the lab.

"You don't fit the mold, my man." Baffled, Rocky punctuates his point with a vigorous "nuh-uh," shaking his head for emphasis. "You ain't a brother... hell, you ain't even *Mexican!*"

Then, throwing up his hands dramatically, he cries, "What the fuck you *doin'* here?"

To help me fit in better, Rocky outfits me with an old white lab coat that he says he "liberated" from some doctor. Presenting me with this cherished uniform on my third day on the job, he announces with great satisfaction, "Now, you one of us!"

With Rocky, I do feel like "one of us." Sometimes we get together on weekends and go into San Francisco to poke around. He introduces me to local landmarks, like Coit Tower. I had heard of, but never seen, the poignant murals painted there some forty years ago, during the Great Depression, by artists employed in the federal government's Works Progress Administration.

Knowing how much I love to read, Rocky makes sure we frequent the fabled City Lights Bookstore, founded by the poet Lawrence Ferlinghetti (after his own military service). We also spend time in the equally — though more dubiously — famous Condor Club in North Beach. This is the bar Carol Doda put on the map as the first topless dancer in the United States.

On the job, Rocky and I always find time to play Teletype Football, one of the first interactive football games. By rigging up teletypes to computers, some local engineers have created an etherworld version of the "Big Game." Crowding around the printer with my fellow lab techs to watch Stanford compete with UC Berkeley, I get the same feeling I had as a kid when I played Foto-Electric Football in the basement of our family home, back in Magnolia. Even in this limited, simulated game, the excitement is palpable when a Stanford back breaks a tackle for a first-down gain or a Cal safety intercepts a long downfield pass.

When the teletype machine clickety-clack and spits out the destinies of the two-dimensional football players, I sometimes feel a touch of *deja vu* — transported back to the basement of Holder Hall, watching the teletype print out numbers on pleats of white pages as I learned my fate, decided as impersonally as the outcome of this game.

My reading habit sets me apart from everyone in the lab. During breaks, especially while I'm waiting for the beakers to finish soaking, I'm able to devour dozens of books. Stuck on this job for the next two years, I decide early on to turn the long, dull hours into an opportunity. For all I learned at Princeton, I'm incredibly ignorant of American literature, so I set myself on a course to catch up. All my lab co-workers notice my devotion to books like *Look Homeward, Angel; East of Eden; For Whom the Bell Tolls; A Farewell to Arms,* and *The 42nd Parallel.*

"What the fuck you doin' wit' that?" Rocky's eyes pop as he grabs my book. Here again, he's imitating what the doctors are thinking.

"Bro, these here doctors don't know what to make of you," he goes on. "They askin', 'Why you washin' my shit?'"

Determined to keep me employed, Rocky often offers me job counseling: "Don't give 'em anything to gnaw on, my man."

"Gnaw on?" I'm confused. "Seems like my being here is something they're gnawing on."

"Keep your head down, bro," he presses. "Let 'em know *they* the bosses. You dig?"

"I dig!" I say. "But y'know, Rocky, I'm not so good at keeping my head down and kissing ass."

"Okay, Mr. CO!" he says with a big grin. "Okay!"

Then he mutters the same line he uses to end all our conversations: "Now you slippin' an' slidin' in that *allllmmmighty* grease!"

Cupping one hand backwards in farewell, he struts out of my office and down the hall, devilishly cackling to himself the whole way.

* * *

We lab techs have a regular lunchtime table on the southern wall of the VA cafeteria, where we often engage in a raucous game of Hearts. The real competition isn't for money; it's for the most memorable line of the day.

When Peri Woods, a diminutive woman whose radical politics make me feel right at home, "Shoots the moon" — getting all 13 hearts *and* the queen of spades — she triumphantly scoops up the last trick while imitating Audrey Hepburn by crooning "Moon River." When one of us tries unsuccessfully to sweep the table, the loser must face the howling cry, "Baby Moon" — a derisive term for taking 25 points, one short of the triumphant 26. Rocky and Michael borrow from Stephen Stills's hit song as we pass our three lousiest cards to the player to the left. "If you can't be with the one you love," Rocky sings gleefully, smirking as he passes his trash to me, "love the one you're with."

Our games attract bystanders, many of whom are veterans. Some ask if they can join. Out of respect for their service, we always give up one of our spots at the table. The vets are of all ages; they've fought in both World Wars, Korea, Vietnam. The youngest aren't much older than I am, and many have lost body parts. I try not to gawk at them, feeling guilty and relieved that I am still whole.

One Vietnam vet tells me about the challenges of adjusting to civilian life, much as my Princeton friend, Ray Butler, described his return. Both counted the days until they would be back home. They use similar words to convey the same thought: "You have no idea how fucked up it was 'in country.' You have no idea how that place fucked me up. Then, we get home and everyone treats us like shit."

All the soldiers are lonely. Eager to pick up scraps of our conversation and teasing, they often linger at our table. Especially Walter.

I have no idea how old Walter is, but to call him grizzled is a kindness. A faded World War II cap covers his long, disheveled gray hair — a far cry from the buzz cut he surely sported as a young Army recruit. Tacked to the left side of his cap is a small pin recognizing his participation in the invasion of Italy.

He looks at me with a perpetual squint, probably attributable to the ubiquitous cigarette hanging from the corner of his mouth. A long, sun-faded scar runs down the right side of his face. Once upon a time, I think, Walter must have been handsome, with his square jaw and wrinkles that dance around his eyes when he smiles.

But now, he looks broken: slouched over, with a pronounced limp. Mostly, he keeps to himself. So, one day — when he comes up to me and says, "Hey, kid, you wouldn't happen to have a smoke, would you?" — I'm startled and a little scared.

Probably noticing my alarm, maybe thinking that he appears menacing, Walter quickly softens his demeanor. "Listen, kid," he drawls, "I ain't gonna do nothing to you."

To cover my unsettled response to him, I involuntarily smile, but I don't know whether to look him in the eye or avert my gaze. Shaking my head, I mutter, "I – sorry, I don't smoke."

"Hey, kid, I just wanna talk to somebody..."

Somebody... like me?

He continues, in a thick drawl, "... and, you know, it helps me if I got some coffin nails in my pocket."

Coffin nails? I feel my brows furrowing. Walter can tell I have no idea what he's talking about.

"You're green, kid, ain't ya?" He smiles kindly. "When I was your age, we got packs of three Camels to keep us goin'." Pulling one last cigarette out of his crumpled pack, he lights up, then thoughtfully blows smoke out of the corner of his mouth, away from me.

"Tell ya what, kid," he says, squinting. "You bring me some Camels every Friday, and I'll tell you stories that'll shrivel your dick. How's that sound?"

Not sure that sounds so great, but I *do* want to hear his stories. So, even though I've never smoked in my life and I'm not tempted to try, I find out where to buy Walter his Camels to keep him talking.

On Friday, instead of playing Hearts, I find Walter, secluded, far across the large cafeteria. Taking a seat across the table from him, I slide two packs of unfiltered Camels in his direction. Walter sweeps his thin, blue-veined arm to the middle of the table and rakes in the cigarettes, as if he's just won a large pot in a poker game. He taps the pack on the table, unwraps the cellophane, releases one, and strikes a match.

"I ain't from around here." He glances up at someone passing by, to make sure he can't hear. "You probably figured that out. I hail from Oklahoma, kid," he semi-whispers, as if he's sharing a shameful secret. "A real honest-to-God Okie. That's what I am."

I think about the Okies in *The Grapes of Wrath* – farm laborers displaced by the Great Depression's dust storms, despised wherever they went. The name came from their cars, parked in the California migrant camps, bearing telltale Oklahoma license plates reading "OK." I wonder if Walter still thinks that an "Okie" conjures up the image of someone driving a battered pickup truck with a pee-stained mattress tied to the roof.

"I know I look like shit, and, for all I know, smell like it, too." Walter sniffs his armpits to make his point and snickers. "I've had my eye on you. I always watch you play cards at the table. You're not like your buddies over there. You're a lot younger. Why're you here?"

There it is again: the question of why I don't fit in. For a moment, I think about whether to tell Walter I'm a CO If I do, I expect he'll get up and leave, taking his cigarettes along. I'll be out 58 cents for the two packs, and I won't get any stories.

But, when I work up the courage to say that I'm doing alternative service here, his response shocks me. "Shit!" he says, leaning over and narrowing his eyes. Then he says through clenched teeth, "I don't blame you one goddamn bit, kid."

"Really?" I can't contain my surprise.

"Look around you. Don't you see these kids? So young, and some of 'em totally fucked up."

"Yeah, I see them," I nod. "It's awful. Sometimes I get so angry that this happened to them. That our country did this to them."

"I know," he spits, and I realize that he's as sick about it as I am. "I can't stand to look at their stumps — the missing fingers, 'n' arms, 'n' legs!"

Then Walter explains that this is what he calls his "last stop." He's got the "Big C," and doctors don't give him much more time.

"Don't got no family around here, so this is it for me." He pauses to take a deep drag on his cigarette. I watch its long cylinder of ash dangling and wonder when it will drop off. I wonder what this dying old man wants from me. Why has he chosen me as the "somebody" he's going to talk to? He's at the end of his life; I'm at the beginning of mine.

But he insists we get together. "Look, kid, just keep playing cards with your pals during the week," he tells me. "And I'll keep watching. Does me good to see some honest bullshitting around here. But on Fridays, you and me, pardner... well, we're gonna spend 'em at this here table."

And we do. At that table, I learn of Walter's impoverished childhood in Tulsa, Oklahoma, of his riding the rails in the late 1930s, looking for work. Eventually, he returned to Tulsa and took up with a good-looking redhead, who broke his heart with a "Dear John" letter after he enlisted.

Walter tells me how dumb he felt as a recruit; how seasick he was on the ship to North Africa, where he fought under General Dwight Eisenhower; how much the soldiers wanted to land in Italy, to fight under Lieutenant General Mark Clark. Clark was known for leading the Fifth Army when it captured Rome in June 1944, around the same time as the Normandy landings.

Walter is steadily chatty, except when he tries to explain how he got his limp. He gets a faraway look in his eyes, and I imagine he's having flashbacks.

"It's hard for me to remember," he says. "It all happened so fast and slow, at the same time. That don't make any sense, but time kind of buckled.

"All's I know is them there fuckers shot me in the left leg. Shot me up pretty good. But those nurses in the hospital, they were real angels. And let me tell you, they were a sight for sore eyes. I didn't care what hospital I went to... long's there were those angels to look at."

After months of delivering Camels to Walter, I'm no longer trading in packs; I'm buying him cartons. It's obvious that he's going down-hill; the cancer in his stomach is eating him alive. Sometimes, I wonder if providing his coffin nails is accelerating his placement in a real coffin — but I also know that smoking is one of the few pleasures he has left. He's not about to change his ways now.

Eventually, Walter can't meet me in the cafeteria anymore. He's too weak to get up, so I visit him at his bedside. At one of our last meetings, he opens his eyes wide, and I can gaze right into his gray-blue irises. He senses that I won't be able to buy many more stories with Camels.

"Kid, I never did learn how to fit in after the war," he admits. He's much more direct now. "Bounced from job to job, woman to woman. Never could settle down. I think that's part of what I brought home from war. That restlessness."

"It's a wound nobody can see," I agree.

"Yeah, and those are much worse than the physical ones," he says. "Don't think you ever heal from those. I'm glad you never had to deal with all that.

"I want to tell you something," he says with some urgency. "Kid, you saved yourself by never going to war. You have no idea what it does to a man. I was never the same."

"Well, the same or not," I tell him, "I'm glad I've gotten to know you. Thanks for telling me your stories, Walter."

"And thanks for the cigarettes," he says softly, reaching out his large hand to shake mine with warmth and affection.

Then, with his thick index finger — the one I've studied as he smokes and gestures — he wipes a tear from his cheek. "One other thing," he says emphatically, mustering all the strength he has left. "You, kid — you got a chance."

He stares out the window at the palm trees blowing in the wind. Then he says gruffly, "Don't fuck it up, now."

For a moment, I'm not sure he's talking to me. But then he turns back to look me in the eye. "You got a chance to do something with your life. You hear me, kid?"

Walter's eyes blaze with a blue fire, and his words blister as he repeats, "Don't fuck it up."

* * *

No longer consumed with studies, having adjusted to the rhythms of an 8-to-4 weekday work schedule, I find myself with plenty of time, particularly on weekends. I'm drawn to the United Farm Workers (UFW), the farmworkers' labor union led by the charismatic Cesar Chavez. His mission is to improve wages and conditions of workers, while adhering to nonviolent action. The UFW has attracted many idealistic young people who are committed to social justice and eager to volunteer their time and energies.

Farmworkers, including children, toil in extreme heat, earning wages even below the legal minimum, and live in substandard temporary housing — all under the supervision of callous agribusiness employers. Worse, they are excluded from the bargaining rights granted to other laborers decades ago, under New Deal legislation. Belatedly, the UFW is organizing this population that has largely been ignored by the labor establishment as well as the general public — in part because most "campesinos" are either Mexican or Filipino.

In the early 1970s, the surging UFW is shifting its efforts toward organizing workers in the California wine industry, which is expanding production as demand for American wines takes off. Vintners need reliable harvest workers to turn out their product, and Chavez has managed to link urban protest to his rural organizing.

Those of us who work for the UFW engage in "secondary boycotts" to help the unionization process. Mostly on weekends, we stand at the entrances of liquor and grocery stores that sell non-UFW products, holding placards, joyfully singing and chanting protest slogans, urging customers to shop elsewhere or, at the very least, to boycott non-UFW wines and table grapes.

"Que viva le huelga!" "Nosotros venceremos!" "Abajo los esquiroles!" We shout, asking customers not to support scab labor. Aiming to reach everyone, we switch between Spanish and English. Long live the strike! We will win! Down with the scabs!

Many customers denigrate our efforts. Some won't even look at us as they enter the stores. Others swear at us, flip us off, even spit on us. One creep tries to bargain with a women protestor: "I won't go into the store if you'll let me feel your boobs."

But when we actually get customers to engage with us, often persuading them to shop elsewhere, we salute them — and ourselves — with cheers and shouts of "Right on!" Over time, more and more people join the secondary boycott; occasionally, rural UFW members demonstrate alongside us to broaden the movement and give our boycott a more "primary" feel.

At the same time, I've been immersing myself in reading the known and unknown giants of American Jewish literature. I'm astonished by the power of Bernard Malamud and Philip Roth. My Princeton friend Jim Lieber writes to me often and recommends Henry Roth's *Call It Sleep.* That book lapsed out of print for nearly thirty years before a new edition was released in the 1960s. A brilliant exploration of immigration, it's an example of how downtrodden people — like the farm workers — often have the answers to our biggest problems.

This reading reminds me of a lesson from my confirmation class about the prophet Amos. A poor shepherd — a farmworker of sorts – Amos, too, demanded social justice; his denunciations of indifference matched the idealistic present-day calls for social change. In fact, my idol, Robert Kennedy, had aligned himself with the farmworkers in

1968. He helped convince Cesar Chavez to end his 25-day fast protesting violence against strikers. And, in an act of solidarity with his fellow Catholic, Kennedy also took communion with Chavez.

Every couple of weeks, I write to Jim, often describing in detail my work with the UFW. His letters back tell me that he's restless and unhappy in law school. He devotes most of his productive hours to writing long journalistic pieces, cracking the law books only when he's near exhaustion.

Jim's efforts produce remarkable results. His powerful article appearing in *The Atlantic* magazine about Rubin "Hurricane" Carter, an African-American boxer wrongfully convicted of murder, is an early contribution to the successful campaign for Carter's exoneration after he had languished in jail for more than twenty years.

In the spring of 1972, Jim writes to say that he's weary of law classes and frustrated that he's not contributing more to changing the real world. He has requested and received a leave of absence from the University of Pennsylvania Law School. In the fall, he writes that he's planning to spend the coming year as an unpaid union organizer for the UFW in the Bay Area.

I'm thrilled to learn of his plans, especially because he'll be nearby — but once he arrives, I don't see much of him. He's putting in 60-hour workweeks coordinating boycotts at various stores, fundraising for the union, and working on establishing the legal rights of farmworkers to organize. Lacking a home base, he often crashes on friends' couches or the floor of church basements. Yet, when we get together occasionally, he tells me that he finds the work for the UFW fulfilling, and he feels a great sense of purpose.

On a rare Sunday afternoon in spring of 1973, when we both have time off from work, we're able to meet at a park in Palo Alto. It's a picture perfect California day, and when I approach the grassy hillside we've designated, I can immediately spot Jim at a distance. I remember his bearing from Princeton — always self-possessed, determined, poised. But when I get closer to him, I see he looks pale. His eyes are heavily lidded, and his face is drawn.

"You doing okay?" I ask as we shake hands and then hug, thumping one another's backs enthusiastically.

"Doing okay." He tosses an arm around my shoulder as we walk toward a spot on a small rise. "But the hours are long, and the accommodations — well, it's not exactly the Nassau Inn back in Princeton. At least they had mattresses."

We settle on a tuft of grass, catching up as we watch children playing on a jungle gym. He tells me he loves working for the UFW, but he knows he can't do it for the rest of his life.

"I'm going back to law school in the fall, Bruce," he says flatly. "I'm not looking forward to it, but I figure I'll need the credential for whatever I'm going to do next."

Shoulder to shoulder, we sit quietly for a few minutes, inhaling the freshly mown grass, falling into our easy companionship. I'm thinking how great it is to have Jim here. I always feel calm and supported when I'm with him, and I'll miss him when he's gone again.

"What about you?" he asks. "You thinking about what you're going to do next?"

"Thinking about it," I shrug. "But I'm really not sure. Working at the lab and for the UFW has changed me."

"Have you reapplied to Stanford?" he asks, and my stomach tightens.

"Nope. I'll never go back to that fuckin' place." I guess Jim is surprised that I'm still so bitter toward Stanford. My face reddens as I remember that Jim, who is so well-spoken, never stoops to profanity to express an idea.

"I get it," Jim says, pulling up a handful of grass and tossing it in the breeze.

"I did contact Santa Clara," I add. "I probably could go there if I want."

"Yeah, okay," Jim says. "But *is* that what you want?"

I don't know what to say, except to answer honestly: "I just don't know."

This is the first time I've admitted out loud that I have conflicted feelings about attending law school. For one thing, I explain, Mr. Cleary has transferred out of state, so I've lost him as a mentor. I haven't been in a classroom for months, and I fear I've lost my academic drive — even the ability to sit passively in a classroom and listen to lectures, or engage in what now seems like lofty, artificial Socratic dialogue.

"Maybe, just maybe —" I think of my pal Rocky – "I'm slippin' away from my life plans, slidin' in that 'almighty grease.'"

"You'd make a helluva lawyer, Bruce, but..." Jim pauses, looking out at clouds drifting slowly across the sky, and then faces me directly. "Look, law school isn't what you think it is. Neither is the law. I had no idea that classes would be so sterile, and the work would be so tedious and dull.

"I don't even know any more if the law is for me. I'm committed to getting the degree, but I don't know... And I'm not so sure I'd recommend it to you."

Glancing away, I hope Jim doesn't see the tears sprouting in the corners of my eyes. Instead, I watch a boy tackle the ladder of the jungle gym, his body hanging and flailing as he struggles to reach the next rung, each more difficult than the last.

"You know, Bruce, this country isn't the same place it was in 1968, when we were back at Princeton. Taking classes with Garvey, trying to decide what area of law was right for us."

I turn back toward Jim as he shrugs. "A lot of what we *were* is just that: past tense! We aren't the same guys we were in college... maybe not even who we were a year ago."

Jim hesitates a little, then manages to look me in the eye. "All I'm saying is that you have a lot to offer." He smiles broadly at me. "Who knows! Maybe your contribution won't be as a lawyer. And you know what?"

"What?" No idea where he's heading.

"That's *okay!*" Then he adds reassuringly. "It's okay."

I study his face, wondering if he can see something that's beyond my vision. He bores his deep, dark eyes into mine and offers simple yet powerful words of guidance.

"Never forget, Bruce: There are lots of ways to serve our country."

"Mr. Wasser! Mr. Wasser!" *"Hey!* Mr. Wasser!"

In Room 460 at Newark Memorial High School, thirty-five juniors surround me and vigorously debate, in front of the American flag, the role of the United States in southeast Asia. We're concluding our study of the Vietnam war in my American History class and — now as then — feelings run high.

Just like a previous generation of young people, my students are deeply divided over the war. Many have relatives who served; others have family members who protested. They reflect and refract those experiences.

I explain how the military draft works, and then I tell my students that I was a conscientious objector — someone who refuses to serve in the armed forces or to bear arms on moral, ethical, or religious principles.

"Wait! So you were a coward who got out of fighting in the war?" One student challenges me aggressively.

"No, no!" Another jumps to my defense. "He was a hero who stood up for what he believed was right!"

As they fiercely debate my character, I almost feel as if I'm on trial. They're asking the same questions I constantly asked myself: "What

241

do I owe my country? What kind of American refuses to serve? What kind of *man* won't fight?"

I hold up a hand to quiet things down. "Let's get to our activity for the day." Looking around at their now-attentive faces, I set the scene: "It's 1969, and we're at Selective Service headquarters in Washington, DC."

We're about to simulate the draft lottery in the classroom. The idea is to help my students understand, in the context of the war, the lottery's random nature, its enormous consequences, and the quandary it created for draft-eligible men. Today's class is an event, and I'm the emcee.

"What – *what*? Mr. Wasser. What's Selective Service?"

"How do we know which one of us gets picked?"

"What if I don't want to fight?"

"Did you say we're having a *lottery*? What's up with that?"

"Today," I announce, in my most authoritative voice, "for the first time in 27 years, the United States has again started a draft lottery."

"Is this another Duber Dude lesson?" One student pipes up from the back of the room. We all laugh; my students have heard so many Martin Duberman stories that he has become a character in our classroom.

"No, no," I answer, "I came up with this one myself. Now settle down, and let's get to work. I'm about to call out lottery numbers, and you're going to find out whether you will have to go to war."

"The last time America had a lottery was in 1942. Now, it's December 1, 1969, and the first pick of the night is September 14. So that birthday is designated 001, which means: For 19-year-olds born on Sept 14, beginning in January, the local draft boards will induct those men first. The next birthdate, April 24th, is 002. December 30 is 003...

"Numbers lower than 120 definitely will be drafted. The middle group — from 120 to 240 — have a 50-50 chance of being drafted next year. The highest-ranking numbers — from 240 to 366 — will probably not be drafted in 1970. However, there may be another lottery in November of next year.

"Today —" I gaze around the room — "all of you are now 19 years old. Please call out your birthdays, and I'll give you your numbers."

I've taught here in Newark, California, a working-class community near Oakland, since the district hired me in 1973, after I finished my two-year alternative military service as a hospital glass cleaner. When I was hired, I traded in my Hondo sideburns for a tightly trimmed beard. Now, my beard, like my hair, has flecks of gray. I'm old enough to be my students' father.

Every day in class renews my love of American history, with all its complexities, contradictions, and possibilities. Here, history is more than a sterile chronology of events; it provides adolescents with the opportunity to make informed moral judgments — not just about the past, but about the way they behave, now and in the future. History is a means to discover each student's voice, ethics, and identity.

When I announce each number and tie it to a birthdate, the class erupts in catcalls and heckling remarks, just like at Princeton so long ago. I tell the students with low numbers to stand on one side of the room. Those who receive high numbers happily vault themselves over desks to the other side. Those with ambiguous numbers remain seated.

A short, blocky Hispanic boy, Jorge Riesco, who combs his hair straight back and always sports sunglasses, has been an outspoken opponent of the war. He shouts out his birthday — July 31st.

"Jorge," I say, "you're number 11."

243

"11!" He crumples in disappointment. "*Chingame!*"

"Loser! Loser!" Jorge's classmates taunt. "Na na na na, na na na na, hey, hey, hey, good-bye!"

"I ain't gonna stick around for this." He waves his hand to snub the group with low numbers.

"So what does that mean?" I ask him. "Where are you going to go?"

"I'm going to Mexico!" he declares, as if that solves his problem.

"Uhhh, Jorge, you do understand what that means?" I present him with his bleak choice. "You'll be evading the draft, what some call a 'draft dodger.' That's a felony, and you can't come back here."

He silently mouths, "Shit!"

"And even if you don't come back," I tell him, "you could have uninvited guests at every family event. Every wedding, every funeral, for years to come. The FBI will track you down to arrest you."

Slowly, his head hanging low, he walks over to join the "losers."

Chauncey Houghton, the son of a Vietnam vet, struts to the opposite side of the room when he learns his draft number is 317. He had argued for increased American involvement in southeast Asia.

"Hey, Chauncey, still gonna tote that gun now?" His classmates press him. "You wanna shoot some VC, dude?" He raises his eyebrows and smiles.

"What do I *do?*" Shannon Morrison moans when she draws 117. "How am I going to play this?"

She looks to her classmates for guidance. During our discussion, Shannon argued that she wouldn't fight in a civil war on the "frickin' other side of the world." In her colorful skirt and boots, she could be right out of the '60s. And she sounds like it, too: "Hell no, I won't go!" she cries from her seat.

When the bell rings, the room clears out, but loud discussion continues among my juniors.

As I'm straightening papers on my desk, Amy Hashimoto approaches me. A thin, reserved student, Amy drew a low number and immediately seemed to carry the weight of it in her entire being. When she took her place with the "losers," she was so humiliated that she wouldn't make eye contact with any of her classmates.

"Mr. Wasser, Mr. Wasser!" she begins. "I don't say this much. In fact, I don't say it at all. I know I'm always critical of America in class."

Amy has engaged in her own ongoing dialogue with US history in journal entries for our class. She often writes eloquently about her admiration of the abolitionists, the Freedom Riders, and Thoreau's "Civil Disobedience." She has argued against American imperialism at the turn of the 20th century, and she's harshly critical of today's consumerist culture. And she's acutely aware of her own family's history, when relatives were sent to "internment" camps during World War II.

Now, dropping her gaze, she says softly, "I actually love America. I love it a lot."

She shakes her head. "My number is 27, but I can't serve," she snaps. "I won't! I can't kill! It's not who I *am*, Mr. Wasser!"

Tears tumble from her hazel eyes. Then she looks up at me and says pleadingly, "Mr. Wasser, this isn't *fair!*"

Our eyes lock, and my stomach churns. Amy can't fully fathom that, three years before she was born, the fates of hundreds of thousands of 19-year-olds rested on a lottery drawing. Their draft numbers confronted American boys with their first adult decision: a defining moral choice that they had to make for themselves. Each had to decide whether to serve; to find a way to dodge the draft, perhaps by leaving the country; or to announce himself to the world as a man incapable of fighting.

The draft lottery on December 1, 1969, upended the lives of many young men, including mine. It's the reason I stand here today, in this lively high-school classroom, proud to be Amy Hashimoto's history teacher.

"I know, Amy." I nod, though that scarcely conveys how my heart aches with empathy.

"I know. It *isn't* fair."

Afterword

In my home office, my framed Princeton diploma hangs on the wall, next to my Phi Beta Kappa and Afro-American Studies certificates. Close by is Martin Duberman's "America" lithograph, next to a 19th-century drawing of the Princeton campus — a gift from a student.

Despite my office decor, my relationship with Princeton remains conflicted. Grateful as I remain for my beloved professors and cherished friends, I've never felt a bond with the university. I was secretly happy when my sons' applications were denied; I didn't want them spending their undergraduate years in the place that caused me so much discomfort and pain. Yet I was thrilled when three Newark students attended Princeton, knowing their diverse ethnic and class backgrounds would enrich its once-homogenous student body.

During my time there, Princeton's unstated mandate was that its "gentlemen" were educated to lead. We were trained to be titans who would run the nation: CEOs, professors, politicians, lawyers, doctors. As a public-school teacher, I fell woefully short.

In the spring of 2023, the Class of '71 contacted me — as it does every year — to solicit membership dues for the alumni group and invite me to join in class activities. I have consistently refused involvement because of the insulting poll that was my classmates' parting shot. Though I had never explained my refusal, this time I happened to speak to a class officer. At last, I told him about my long-standing hurt at being labeled the guy who considered himself smarter than anyone else. This sparked a discussion among Class of '71 committee members, and an officer located the offending poll.

I hadn't remembered exactly what the poll said. But when the officer sent me a copy, I saw that the three-page-long list was silly, sophomoric, and not at all funny. In fact, given that no classmates remembered filling out a questionnaire, it's unlikely there *was* a poll. The yearbook editors and their friends probably compiled the list for cheap laughs. It was a particularly cruel byproduct of Princeton's prankster culture.

Later that year, more than half a century after the hurtful poll appeared, the Class offered me an apology: "On behalf of the Princeton Class of '71, we wish to formally apologize for a negative depiction of you that was published under the title of a "Senior Class Poll-1971" in the Class of '71 *Nassau Herald*... It is understandable that you and your family were negatively impacted by the words that appeared in the Class publication. The Class finds those words distasteful and wishes to express great regret for their publication... It is the sincere hope of current Class leadership that this apology will relieve some of the negative feelings you have held over the years toward the Class of '71 and will encourage you to engage with the Class in any ways that feel comfortable to you. We consider you, Bruce Wasser, to be a valued and respected member of the Princeton Class of '71."

In its own small way, the Class of '71 thereby involved itself in the larger, ongoing national conversation about historical responsibility.

Though I'm grateful for these initial steps, words alone are insufficient. Atonement also calls for action.

I suggested that the Class sponsor a Princeton program to combat bullying, but the officer said the university already has numerous programs that strive to create a supportive, inclusive community. I then recommended that the Class of '71 donate to Newark Memorial High School, to help fund a program that opposes prejudice and educates students about the lingering damage of bullying. Unfortunately, no further action has been taken.

Quiet, determined protest has been a guiding principle of my life. Over the years, I involved myself in movements supporting justice for farmworkers, racial equity, reparations for Japanese Americans interned during World War II, and gender equality. I risked my teaching career by denouncing a vicious, patently homophobic California initiative.

My most significant societal contribution — reflecting my dedication to protest and resistance — was becoming a teacher. In my classroom, surrounded by my beloved students, I worked every single day at encouraging these young people to find their own voices, to stand for principle, to be unafraid to challenge wrong. I felt obligated to help them become compassionate, empathetic, dedicated citizens.

Every teacher enters a classroom with an agenda. Mine was to bend the moral arc of the universe closer to justice.

In one of life's great ironies, I maintained a relationship with the Selective Service System, chairing our local draft board for 15 years. I volunteered out of gratitude for the fair treatment I received, as well as my belief that the presence of a CO on the board was a strong statement that would help other applicants believe they, too, were receiving a fair hearing. While I was proud of my service to the draft board, I'm convinced that it would be more equitable if the United States required compulsory national service — military or non-military — for *all* young adults.

In my family, all our relationships were deeply affected by the stress of those tumultuous years in the late 1960s and early 1970s. Thankfully, my sister, Adrienne, and I have been able to sustain a lifelong bond. After completing her peripatetic educational journey — three high schools, two universities — she remained in the San Diego area, establishing herself as a successful advisor for college applicants.

Sweet, gentle Cindy never recovered from the devastation of losing our father. Floundering as a student, she perpetually bounced from one job, one relationship, one crisis to another. Hindered by our six-year age difference and the devastation of our father's death, I was never able to be a loving and present brother to our "wild child." She died when she was 32, a passenger in a drunk-driving accident, just before I turned 40.

Even after I finished my alternative service and began my teaching career, my mother never again mentioned my CO status. She never forgave me for forfeiting my dream of becoming a lawyer; she was deeply disappointed that I chose teaching, and her displeasure further strained our relationship.

Mom dated several men who had lengthy military careers, but she never remarried. I believe life crushed her, and I have long since forgiven her cruel remarks. I now know they were uttered out of fear, loneliness, and disappointment.

I also know that ours was not the only family fractured by the politics of the time. Parents and children across the country hotly debated America's involvement in southeast Asia; often they found themselves unable to bridge their opposing views. Sadly, damaged families were yet another price of the Vietnam war.

I hope this memoir provides insight into how a young man's life can be shaped, even devastated, by his father's untimely death. For me, losing Dad at 15   then having to face the hardest moral decision of my young adult life without his guidance — magnified my loss and intensified my search for surrogate father figures.

I'm grateful to those who offered paternal counsel: Uncle Alex; Coach Dick Eiler; Professors Martin Duberman, Eric Goldman, and Gerald Garvey; my Stevenson mentors, Caddie and Cleve; my friends, especially Jim and Walter; and even men I knew only from their public personas, including Robert F. Kennedy and Dr. Martin Luther King. Even when our ideas didn't agree, all modeled what it means to stand for something, what it means to have conscience and convictions, what it means to be a man. They picked up where Dad left off.

In recent decades, I have come to peace with the death of my father. I still feel the void he left — yet, when I taught, I felt his presence in my classroom work. Like him, I was an affectionate, kind, large-spirited man who stepped in as a father figure to students who needed one. Also like Dad, I developed a sense of humor that I often directed against myself. I coached two high-school championship softball teams, and my ballplayers called me "Skip" — just what I called Dad when I played for him. Now, he's beside me every spring when, as an umpire in Lake Bluff, I yell, "Play ball!"

The most important reason I wrote 90 – which I see as an American story of idealism and moral ambiguity — is to encourage anyone facing a crisis of conscience and its consequences. I want to offer support and solace to those who choose a path of resistance — whether by becoming an activist in a political cause; challenging harassment in social media or the workplace; honoring a difficult commitment, or defying family, peer, and cultural pressures to follow their convictions.

Today, college campuses are erupting in dissent over distant wars; there are marked similarities and differences between these protests and those of 50 years ago. Now and then, students are raising their voices in hopes of changing the world. Their discontent, like ours decades ago, tests the limits of the First Amendment.

However, protests against the Vietnam War differed from the outcry against the war in the Mideast. During my youth, students, heavily influenced by the nonviolent civil disobedience of the civil rights movement, rarely engaged in acts of aggression. We marched, chanted, and organized, always hoping our actions would *persuade* others to join us. Today's activists often mock nonviolent civil disobedience; occasionally their provocative language, knowingly or unknowingly, feeds ancient prejudices and threatens First Amendment protections.

Serious issues plague all of us today: racism, prejudice, environmental degradation, societal violence, the proliferation of guns, police brutality, assaults on reproductive rights, gender-identity issues. The list goes on and on. So must the fight.

When it comes to these struggles, none of us can be conscientious objectors.

Acknowledgments

Two decades ago, I told this story to my wife, Fern Schumer Chapman, who suggested that I should write about it, both to ease my own pain and to offer solace, hope, and guidance to others. It was her loving support and incomparable professional guidance that brought it about.

I want to thank Susan Figliulo for expert editing. Her contributions are significant, but invisible to the reader. Her fingerprints are on every page.

Friends and family offered encouragement and constructive criticism. Paul Basbagill, whom I have known for over twenty years, supported my efforts; even though this memoir does not focus on the Chicago White Sox, I feel somewhat confident Paul will forgive that omission. Bruce Storrs and Steve Jennings, Clairemont High School classmates, rekindled memories of my adolescence and shared their impressions of Coach Eiler. My multi-talented sister, Adrienne Behrens, provided crucial insights into our family dynamics. My two sons, Lysha and Elie, enjoyed following the progress of this book and offered their own ideas about its themes.

About the Authors

BRUCE JAY WASSER, a father and grandfather, is retired and living with his wife, Fern Schumer Chapman, in northern Illinois.

FERN SCHUMER CHAPMAN is the author of several award-winning books, including *Motherland,* which was a finalist for the National Jewish Book Award and a Barnes & Noble Discover selection, among other honors. Her other works include *Is It Night or Day?* and *Brothers, Sisters, Strangers.* A sought-after speaker, she has presented to schools, libraries, charity events and women's organizations.

www.fernschumerchapman.com

Credit: Princeton University Yearbook, Class of '71

For Book Clubs

1. What would you have done if you had been in Bruce's shoes and your number was 90?
2. How did Bruce's relationship with his mother reflect the effect of the war on family relationships? Could you identify with her fears and her desires?
3. Given the political divide today, what can we learn from Bruce's and Eiler's relationship?
4. What did each important man in the book – Garvey, Duberman, Goldman, Uncle Alex, Jim, Ric, Eiler, Walter – give Bruce? Why were they crucial to the story?
5. Wars often leave personal and social echoes. What echoes did the Vietnam War leave?
6. How would you evaluate Bruce's experiences at Princeton? Did the memoir alter your impressions of an "Ivy League" education?
7. Bruce was a blue-collar worker both during and after his university experiences. How did his work change his life?
8. Although"90" is very much a book that deals with masculinity and masculine decisions, women have an important place in the memoir. How did women influence Bruce, and what role did they play in his life?
9. Analyze the role of African-Americans in "90." Does the memoir leave the reader hopeful or despairing about the possibilities of a multi-racial society?
10. How do teachers' influence students? What does "90" tell us about the role of educators in Bruce's life and in society?
11. How does the loss of Bruce's father shape the memoir?
12. One of the recurrent themes of American literature is the role of the outsider. In what ways is Bruce an "outsider"? How does he compare to other outsiders in literature and American culture?

13. How does "90" make you reflect on what it means to be a good citizen? Does Bruce match your definition of good citizenship?
14. "90" explores the meaning of "being a man." In what ways is manhood treated in the memoir? Has the definition of manhood changed over the decades since the 1960s?
15. Bruce feels a need to serve his country. In your opinion, what does "serving one's country" mean? Should we adopt this concept today? If so, how?
16. Analyze the role Jim Lieber has in Bruce's life. Is there a comparable person in your own life?
17. What is your opinion about conscientious objectors?
18. In the afterword, Bruce states his approval of requiring all young adults to serve the nation in some manner for two years. What are your thoughts about this proposal?
19. If you had been on San Diego's draft board, what questions would you have asked Bruce to prove his claim of conscientious objection to war?
20. What are your thoughts about war and warfare? Is there a war that you would have refused to fight in? One that you would have volunteered for?

www.ingramcontent.com/pod-product-compliance
Lightning Source LLC
Chambersburg PA
CBHW061142120626
46546CB00005B/1897